*'A new simple solution'*

# Mental Health for Kidz
## (teens & adults)

## 'A new simple solution'

*'A new simple solution'*

# Mental Health for Kidz

## (teens & adults)

### 'A new simple solution'

*Published by MHFK Publishing*

*ISBN 9798396473300*

*Copyright Ó MHFK Publishing 2023*

*A CIP record is available for this book from the British Library*

*The moral right of the author has been asserted*

*Printed in Great Britain by MHFK Publishing*

**6**

*'A new simple solution'*

# Contents

*'A new simple solution'*

*'A new simple solution'*

# Authors Note

This book is the result of a forty-five year journey studying a vast range of subject matter on the workings of the human mind.

The journey incorporated topics such as psychology, self-help, mental health, wellbeing, self-awareness, personal development, depression, bullying, meditation, peak performance, various religions, energy healing, shadow work, emotional health, NLP, hypnotherapy plus many other related subjects.

As well as walking the path of life and being fully immersed in the range of experiences inevitable including a number of mental health issues, as I progressed through the years.

It's a tough journey at times for all of us and for some unknown reason I have always been fascinated by how this journey can be made easier.

A sort of calling to work it all out and this has driven me now for the best part of my life. I have tried just about everything to improve my life in every respect, materially, mentally, physically, emotionally and spiritually and in the pursuit of this goal I have learned so much.

And I have actually succeeded in many areas but I believe this is a never ending process; there is always another step forward you can take. I guess this is the point of it all to learn and grow as you progress through life.

However at this stage of my journey the fog is finally dispersing enough that I can now see much more clearly.

And guess what?

The secrets to life are a lot simpler than I ever thought. And it seems you must tread this long arduous path alone as you work your way to this realisation.

There are no shortcuts, at least none that I am aware of.

So you have to traverse all terrains and go through all the experiences of life to seek out and truly know the truth.

And of course no two journeys are the same, so it's a unique path to you that only you will walk.

I guess this is the beauty of it all.

It really is a personal journey of the soul and my hope is that my experience can maybe benefit and help you in some way.

I have tried my best to explain what I have learned in simple terms and hopefully this will make this book more accessible and useful to more people.

However if only one person has their journey improved in some way by reading my book then I will have succeeded.

And please note this book is about a new approach to the mental health crisis with a focus on the younger generation, absolutely 'yes' but it is also a useful tool for adults that may need a fresh approach and as a by-product it is also I believe a helpful guide on how to walk the path.

The two go in hand so to speak.

This book is available on Amazon in kindle and paperback formats at a nominal price of £1.99 and £5.99 respectively.

It would be helpful if people bought a copy of course but I don't want that to stop people having access to this book, so I have also made if <u>free.</u>

The sold copies will help pay for the free copies because I believe in this work and don't want it to be out of reach for anyone, this way everyone can have the chance to read it, if they so desire of course.

Free copies will be sent out weekly to organisations that predominantly work with young people in the mental health field.

As well as related charities, psychologists, schools, colleges, mental health practices, life coaches, private individuals and any other organisations connected to this genre.

And because we have an electronic PDF version it can be sent anywhere in the world so we will endeavour to do just that.

Anyway I hope you enjoy the book and I wish you the best of luck on your own unique and amazing journey.


Bon voyage!

# Preface

The world is currently in the grip of the worst pandemic in history, 'the mental health pandemic' and this is taking its toll on children and young people like nothing ever seen before. Latest statistics say 10% of children in the UK are now experiencing mental health problems.

There are unprecedented amounts of suicides, mental breakdowns, cases of depression, anxiety, drug abuse, self-harming, eating disorders, alcoholism, ADHD, bullying and many other issues erupting like wildfires within the younger generation.

This plague is wreaking havoc across the world and young lives and families are suffering the consequences, as it scythes through the younger generation like a hot knife through butter.

The repercussions are horrendous as it infects and reaches deep into society at some point inevitably touching every one of us.

Nobody goes unscathed and it seems impossible to stop with governments and health services stretched to breaking point due to the utter magnitude of it all.

And not only the young but people of all ages are crying out for help as the world desperately searches for answers.

This book I hope offers something of a lifeline because it brings a new way, a new perspective, explained I believe simply enough so that virtually anyone reading it should be able to gain a better understanding of what is happening.

This candid viewpoint empowers the reader to be able to make a stand and hopefully in their own case at least, go some way to stopping this pandemic in its tracks.

Knowledge is key here but for it to be beneficial and effective on a large scale it has to be basic and simplistic enough, which I hope and feel has been achieved. This plague of the mind can be beaten and turned back but we must spread the word how to as many people as possible if we are to achieve this.

And we must come to a common understanding of what we are up against and then apply practices that can begin turning the tide. It starts with you, and after reading this book you will know what you can do to get the ball rolling. It really comes down to one simple thing that requires a little effort and that is change yourself and show others how to do the same.

*'A new simple solution'*

# Introduction

*'You must be the change you wish to see in the world'*

## -Mahatma Ghandi

It's actually very easy to change your life for the better and in the process address many of the mental health issues that lots of us are facing.

All you have to do is understand in a simple enough way what is going on inside of you and then have an easy to implement practice to follow, that will change what is going on inside of you.

This is because the life you are immersed in and experiencing is a direct reflection of what is inside of you, so to change the outside you need to change the inside.

I know to some this may sound a little far fetched but if you do some research you will soon find many revered teachings confirming this line of thought, even Buddha said this over 2500 years ago:

*'Since everything is a reflection of our minds, everything can be changed by our minds'.*

## -Buddha

---

**15**

So let's get started, coming back to the present times all across the world right now all we seem to hear about is 'mental health' it has become one of the hottest topics of this era.

And it appears just about everyone is suffering from it in one way or another with new problems being identified and labeled virtually by the day.

It is fast becoming a global health crisis which appears to be out of control and the world it appears is struggling to cope.

I am not disagreeing with this assessment however I believe in general the answer is not so complicated and this 'mental health crisis' that affects all of us in one way or another can be turned around if we understand and approach it in the right way and when we do that our lives will change dramatically for the better.

So the more people that gain a simple understanding of why this is happening and how it can be corrected the better because this is the core controlling factor that determines every aspect of your life.

And of course some mental health problems may be due to conditions not covered by this approach but in general I believe the solution given in this book will help in the majority of cases.

**16**

So before I explain what this 'mental health crisis' is and then look at how changing what's going on inside of you is the solution, I want to alter your perspective slightly and give you an alternative way to view it all.

# Chapter 1

*'If you want to find the secrets of the Universe, think in terms of energy, frequency and vibration'.*

**-Dr Nicola Tesla**

So what is really going on?

The first thing I would like you to understand is that you live in a world that is in fact made up of energy.

Yes that's right everything you see around you including your physical body is actually energy, which in its basic form is atoms, which consists of a nucleus with protons and neutrons whizzing around the centre, these microscopic atoms are pulsing and vibrating. The house you live in, the car you drive, trees, furniture, food, animals etc are all made up from these tiny particles, any scientist or physicist will confirm this. So if you are made from energy (atoms) and all energy vibrates then at some level you must be vibrating?

This is correct; you are constantly vibrating even though you can't directly sense this happening, although you can indirectly sense it through the fluctuation of your moods as you go through your day.

**18**

One minute you may be happy and feeling joyful the next you may get some bad news and suddenly feel down and depressed.

This happens all the time as you encounter the ups and down's of everyday life. This is you sensing your energy vibration, through the way that you feel.

When you feel good you are vibrating fast and when you feel bad your energy vibration is slowing down.

That makes sense because fast vibrating feelings are joy, excitement, happiness, peacefulness and love etc and slow vibrating feelings are anger, fear, anxiety, depression, jealousy, greed etc. So the spectrum range of feelings goes from fast vibrating 'love' down to slow vibrating 'fear' with all the variations in between.

So you can see how it works and why everyday of your life you experience many different positive and negative feelings as you ride up and down on the vibrational roller coaster ride.

It's a muti-vibrational energy experience in every sense of the word and the reason I want you to understand this is because in the next chapter I will explain how your emotions are also energy and how they play a massive role in determining how every aspect of your life works out.

**19**

If you follow the practice of maintaining the state of awareness that everything is energy, then you will see why keeping yourself in as high a vibration as possible is extremely beneficial to you in every conceivable way.

This new way of thinking and being, is called high vibrational thinking.

*'Everything is energy and that's all there is to it. Match the frequency of the reality you want and you cannot help but get that reality. It can be no other way'.*

**-Albert Einstein**

*'A new simple solution'*

# Chapter 2

*'90% of all the pain we experience is due to emotional baggage, trapped emotions and those energies stay with us and cause much of our diseases and self-sabotage'.*

**-Dr Bradley Nelson**
(The Emotion Code)

## Trapped emotions

Next I want you to understand that essentially as soon as you are born you are compromised through the genes you inherit and then the immediate environment that you are born into. This is because of the trapped emotional energies contained initially within the inherited genes and then, that you accumulate through the experiences that you encounter as you are growing up.

Generally this involuntary programming happens mainly in the first seven years of your life when you are very receptive to what's going on around you and acting like a sponge in terms of readily soaking up the energies that you are subjected to. So when you are in the vicinity of other people who have powerful negative emotional moments, like heated arguments filled with anger, exasperation, frustration and fear etc, some of the energy generated can unfortunately become absorbed by you.

**21**

And this can leave you with some of that emotional energy trapped inside of you, which builds up and adds to the residue that you have already accumulated.

Trapped emotions passed on down through your genes is known as epigenetics and this is the same for everybody, it's nobody's fault, it's just how we are all influenced or you could say programmed.

Even the close people to you such as family, neighbours and friends etc, are operating under the affects of their residue of negativity and have no idea when they display highly charged negative emotional states, that you could inadvertently take on board some of those energies.

Many other experiences add to this residue of energy such as living in an atmosphere of worry, stress, unhappiness, poverty, unworthiness, hate and fear etc.

And eventually this 'stuck emotional energy', this reservoir of sludge will begin manifesting through you and this is when it can cause you to react instinctively when similar negative circumstances pop up again. In other words you automatically start behaving in a similar way (getting angry, frustrated, worried etc) when triggered, solidifying the trapped emotions even further in the process, which just keeps them firmly trapped within you.

**22**

This is how your personality begins to form and this is all part of you being molded by the emotional energy that you have involuntarily inherited and encountered into the person you will be.

When the bulk of the energy you are habitually experiencing is predominantly negative, which is usually the case as currently it is estimated that the average person's thoughts are 80% negative in nature and 95% repetitive, it can become the dominant energy form displayed by you, potentially manifesting in a number of different ways.

Such as making you prone to angry outbursts, mood swings, even violent behaviour, sulks, addictive tendencies, severe bouts of anxiety, depression, argumentative, self-pitying, antagonistic, bullying, self-harming, arrogant, vindictive, predatory tendencies, a worrier, stress head etc.

Plus many more negative behaviour patterns and traits that humans can fall into. It could manifest through you in any of these ways depending on your personality type, genes, sensitivity level, previous experiences, etc. When this happens essentially this means your trapped emotional energy is expressing itself through you and this keeps you stuck in a more negative vibrational place.

And this energy spectrum or range is generally where you will spend the majority of your life because you will be monitored by your inner negativiey (inner gremlin), on a daily basis as it triggers you from within to provide it with a steady dose of negative emotional energy.

So the negativity you carry within determines where (vibrationally) you will spend most of your time and ultimately your life will be constantly tainted by the most dominant energies contained within this mix.

This is the major factor that defines you and this also determines how difficult your life path will be and a lower vibrational type of upbringing (full of negative energy) would certainly be very influential in making you a more negatively minded person and potentially lead to a more unhappy life filled with problems.

And this massively affects your mental health increasing your chances of suffering in some way. Although it should be also said you can still have mental health problems even if your childhood is spent in a very positive environment. It's not quite as simple as a high vibrational upbringing means no mental health issues and a low vibrational upbringing means lots of mental health issues but it is a fair indication in most cases.

There are lots of other factors at play but essentially this is how it works. And I am not saying this book will help everyone but I do believe in the majority of cases it will help. So please read with fair discernment and common sense taking the information on board and using what you feel may be beneficial.

Now back to the accumulation of trapped emotions, which would essentially be holding you down at a slower more negative vibration than where you would be naturally, if you didn't have it.

This would cause you to experience in general the corresponding more negative life that is in harmony with this lower vibrational state of mind. You would be stuck in a vibrational place where potentially you have much more chance of developing mental health problems.

On the other hand if you grow up in a loving, joyful, happy home with lots of positive energies around such as joy, fun, thoughtfulness, caring, love etc and you don't inherit much negativity through your genes, then you will generally exist at a fairly high vibration.

This will be the energy spectrum or range that you from then on usually display and spend the majority of your time in.

---

**25**

From this you can see how important and influential your parents, family, friends and the immediate environment that you happen to be brought up in are.

If you are fortunate enough to have very high vibrational parents with little inner negativity to pass on down to you and you are surrounded by other happy positive people you will reap the benefits.

This ensures that you will tend to be in general more positive in nature and your life will have much more chance of being happy and content. And again in respect of your mental health this will decrease your chances of suffering with problems.

Its no coincidence that many people that have a loving, positive, happy upbringing go on to have successful and happy lives, they have less getting in the way. They are fortunate enough to be carrying a smaller less influential and damaging ball of inner negativity, so in effect they have ended up with fewer inner demons to contend with, they have a less powerful gremlin messing with them from the inside.

Like energy attracts like energy so dependant on the amount of inner negativity you have accumulated determines what you will naturally draw into your life, the type of partner, job, friends, wealth, health etc.

**26**

So in general what is inside of you is what you gravitate to on the outside. The more trapped emotions you are carrying (the bigger your gremlin) the more you will attract people and circumstances with a similar amount or a gremlin of similar size.

And although you pick up many of your trapped emotions during the hyper sensitive early years, you also pick them up as you go through your life, especially when you have highly charged intense emotional experiences such as going through a divorce, a job loss, relationship breakups, serious accidents, severe illness, bereavement etc, so as you can see it's always an ongoing process.

And when you go through one of these highly charged intense emotional experiences it can be so distressing that you may suffer what is referred to as PTSD (Post traumatic stress disorder), which basically means you have experienced an exceptionally severe drop in vibration due to the severity of what you have been through.

Or put another way you have suddenly taken on board an unprecedented and large amount of slow vibrating negative energy and this has plunged or dragged you down the vibrations, leaving you stuck even further down than usual in an extreme negative state.

Your gremlin has gorged itself on the negativity generated and rapidly increased in size and power.

This is when you may see a person really start to struggle to maintain their lives, which could even lead to extreme outcomes like homelessness, alcoholism, drug addiction, a fall into crime; relationship breakdowns, serious ill health etc, and in a worst case scenario even develop suicidal tendencies.

The exceptional drop in vibration is just too much to cope with and they desperately need to find relief from the overwhelming and foreboding feelings that are now engulfing them.

If you find yourself trapped in the lower vibrations and it is even more intense if it has suddenly happened to you, then you will experience the energies that exist there and the further down you are the worse it is and this will spill out infecting every area of your life.

You are a totally different person depending on where your vibration has settled.

And this is why we see many people who are trapped down here behaving in ways that may seem massively out of character.

They cannot help how they act because they are now essentially a totally different person and the majority of us would be influenced to behave in exactly the same way if we were in their shoes.

So please don't be too quick to judge others because you don't really know where they are vibrationally and they may well be trapped in a very difficult state of mind through no fault of their own.

They will need all the help, love and understanding they can get to overcome this.

They need help to get them back up the vibrations and this is easier said than done.

# **Chapter 3**

*'Let's raise children who won't have to recover from their childhoods'*

### -**Pam Leo**
An independent scholar in human development, a parent educator, a certified childbirth educator, a doula, a parent, and a grandparent

## Mental health

Now let's look at how this relates to your mental health.

Accumulating a residue of negative energy is just part of life and something that you have to contend with. Everyone has it; some only have a small amount and others a large overpowering amount, but all have it. Essentially this is the after effects of all the traumas small or large that you have faced and gone through throughout your life.

From the extreme example of a loveless abusive childhood to something that may be perceived as less damaging such as someone calling you names (bullying), or maybe just been involved in a severe heated argument, losing a loved one, having a serious accident, suffering neglect, rejection, ill health etc.

I could go on and on there are endless examples.

These traumas and mini-traumas can take many forms and we have all experienced them many times over (it's simply the up's and down's of life) and this is what has left us with trapped negative emotions.

Other factors can also contribute to this such as what we may have inherited in our genes, our personality type (a sensitive soul may suffer much more emotional damage than a more hardy soul for example).

**And this accumulated residue of negativity is what I believe causes the majority of mental health problems.**

Remove your trapped emotions (inner negativity) or inner demons, your gremlin and you would remove the majority of mental health issues that human beings suffer from. In fact existing in this state of being where you are heavily influenced by your inner gremlin has become so 'normal', so accepted that most of the time we don't even realise or question what is happening.

You only think that the people who are seriously malfunctioning are the ones with problems but that is not the case we are all affected all of the time to some degree.

And in general we manage to stumble and fumble through our lives carrying this burden without giving too much attention to it.

However we could all have a much better and easier life if we sorted this problem out and were able to release some of this negativity.

This would allow us to rise in vibration and live our lives in a higher vibrational state where negative energy or our inner gremlin would not be able to play havoc with and hurt us so much.

Unfortunately for some who are carrying a lot of negativity it can become unbearable and it does so much damage they have a miserable life full of problems and dramas, I am sure we all know many people like that.

When you are carrying a lot of negativity it flares up constantly, powerfully infecting your life and the lives of others around you. The symptoms of carrying a strong powerful dose of negative energy varies from person to person.

It may make one person act as a bully, another could suffer from depression and another may end up hooked on drugs or alcohol or even experience lots of ill health.

It all depends on your personality traits, your genes and the behaviour patterns you have been exposed to.

And you could even grow up with a brother or sister and they seem unphased by that same upbringing whereas you are devastated by it.

Everybody is different and we all react differently to our experiences it's not an exact science but generally this is how it works.

The bottom line is the ball of trapped negative energy that we all have stuck within us our inner gremlin is what is causing the majority of our problems.

And it constantly replenishes itself topping up its battery when it triggers negative emotional surges through us. This is how it stays charged up and strong by every now and again flaring up.

And when this happens you become that energy, like when you feel a surge of anger and become angry or when you feel yourself sinking down into misery and become depressed.

It is controlling you and you think it's you but it's not you, it is the trapped emotions you have stuck inside of you flaring up, your inner gremlin living through you.

---

**33**

It's a great way to understand this trapped energy, picturing it as a little gremlin inside of you; you can even give it a name and as I said previously the bigger and more powerful it is the more havoc it will be creating in your life.

The prisons and mental institutions are full of people with powerful inner gremlins.

The gremlin is why a person who bullies people is never satisfied they always need to move on to the next person to bully because their gremlin needs more negative emotional energy, it wants its food and if it doesn't keep getting replenished it will fizzle away so its always seeking the next meal, the next opportunity.

In truth it's the gremlin that's bullying people not so much the 'bully', the gremlin is the driving force behind the 'bully's' cruel actions.

Take the gremlin away and the 'bully' would suddenly stop bullying people. They would no longer be prompted and urged from within to behave in this way.

The same applies to the depressed person, the drug addict, the alcoholic, the person who self-harms or has anxiety issues etc, in other words most of the mental health issues we see occurring are gremlin driven urges.

---

**34**

It's the repetitive and never ending routine of satisfying the gremlin within that always needs its next fix, which it gets through your negative emotions.

When you feel guilty, angry, sad, worthless, jealous, depressed, unloved, self-pitying etc you are feeding your inner gremlin and it gets you to feel like this by encouraging you to drink, take drugs, bully someone, feel jealous, hate yourself, hate others etc.

Whatever way it has found works best to get you in a negative emotional state it will constantly use to feed on the emotions this generates within you.

It negatively taints your thinking because it is there; if it is part of you, it will infect you. And it will learn how to push the exact buttons it knows will do the job and you will then automatically react giving it what it wants every time.

Yes it is even said it carries a primitive form of intelligence and knows how to intentionally manipulate you and encourage you into negative mindsets; as I pointed out previously many ancient teachings refer to this inner energy source as your inner demons and there are many stories of people being driven to despair by them.

And their greatest strength is you not knowing they are there but not anymore because now you know.

Now you are empowered with the knowledge of how it works and this is the first important step in you gaining control.

The fact that you now understand how it works and can acknowledge the presence of your inner gremlin puts you back in the driving seat. And this is crucial in order for you to be able to do something about it.

This enables you to then recognise its promptings when they occur and this is a vital step on the road to you finally releasing the trapped negative energy that is damaging your life.

There is no going back now that you have an understanding of what is taking place and its now time to give notice to the parasite that has covertly been sabotaging your life.

From here on I will refer to this collective residue of negative energy, as your inner gremlin to make it easier for you to see what needs to be done. And in respect of addictive habits such as drugs and alcohol you may also get chemically hooked making it even more difficult to overcome the real problem, which is of course as always the inner gremlin.

# Chapter 4

*'I am absolutely convinced it is our trapped emotions and traumas and anxieties and unprocessed life experiences that we hold in our nervous system that is the source of everything that ails us'.*

**-Sonia Choquette**
(Founder of 6th Sensory Living and Author)

## Summary

So let's presume you are born basically pure and negative energy free (although it is thought you may carry some negativity from your experiences within the womb or even passed on down through your genes).

Then it all begins as you enter your family and immediate environment and begin experiencing negative emotional flare ups and various interactions with your parents, siblings, family, friends, neighbours, TV, etc.

This subjects you to those energies and as you process them some of the residue starts becoming trapped within you and you are then on the way to forming your own ball of inner negativity or your own inner gremlin.

*'A new simple solution'*

Then when you have enough of this energy stuck inside of you its influence causes you to start instigating negative interactions and having negative emotional flare ups and you are then adding to the mix of energies in your immediate environment.

This means you have become part of the cycle unknowingly damaging yourself and others in your close vicinity.

This is why it is so important to bring children up in the best possible energy environment as the pathways they will take in their lives literally is in general determined by the early years energy that they predominantly spend their time in.

I can't stress the importance of this enough because if you have no control over the energy environment so much unnecessary damage can be done.

And because of this phenomenon everybody is essentially suffering from 'mental illness' to some degree (or you could say suffering from the presence of an inner gremlin) and for some it's not too bad, even acceptable and hardly noticeable but for others it's intolerable.

This without doubt is the most powerful overriding factor that we have to contend with in our lives.

It affects literally everything and I mean everything, our relationships, work life, the amount of success we can achieve, our health etc, nothing is untouched by this.

So the cure is obvious 'get rid of what is causing the problem' and that is the negative energy each of us is carrying within, the alien that has took up residence, the gremlin.

Then you would rise in vibration and your life would be changed instantly and massively for the better in every conceivable way.

You see the higher the vibration that you can attain and hold the more happiness, joy, fun, good fortune and love etc, you will experience in your life.

You are a different and much more positively orientated person when you exist at a higher vibration.

Everything seems to work out for the better and things just go your way and you are less bothered by the problems of life because you have less negativity inside of you blowing it all out of proportion.

It's as if you can simply let the relentless daily niggles go without buying into them and when you are in a higher vibrational state this all comes quite naturally to you.

---

**39**

You are automatically instinctively responding to life rather than emotionally reacting when you have a small less powerful inner gremlin.

You will of course still have your ups and downs but much less severe in terms of the damage you suffer than if you were continuously dragged down by the burden of a heavier slow vibrating powerful ball of inner negativity.

I also feel that you need to be careful of extensive therapy digging into the past to find out why someone has 'mental health' issues as a method of releasing them, because this can sometimes simply regurgitate the pain and suffering, which could potentially leave you with an even more powerful inner gremlin than before.

It makes more sense to me to accept the fact that we have damage (everybody does) and simply focus on releasing that pain (the inner gremlin) using techniques that are designed to do that.

Everyone goes through stuff which in general is unknowingly inflicted upon them by people who are behaving that way because they are damaged themselves, so why not just focus on getting rid of that stuck energy and concentrate on healing.

**40**

I feel its not about 'who done what to me' because we all got damaged, its more productive to accept that unfortunately it has happened and concentrate on getting rid of it (the stuck energy), it's just part of the experience that we call life.

Nobody would knowingly hurt you or subject you to negative emotional energy if they carried no inner pain themselves.

They are also suffering and it's their inner pain that causes them to lash out and behave in ways that may inadvertently negatively impact and hurt others.

Realising this and detaching from the negativity involved is the answer, so take your thoughts away from anyone that you feel may have been responsible and let them get on with it, they have their own path to tread and lessons to learn.

Dwelling on it keeps you stuck in their pain so it's best for you to let it go and move on.

If you get caught up in negative thoughts and feelings such as seeking revenge, blaming or falling into the habit of churning over what someone may have done to you, you are fuelling your inner gremlin, you are feeding it.

This kind of mindset is only hurting you more and if you persist in this line of thought your gremlin could grow even stronger giving it more influence over you.

Then it will most certainly cause more chaos and damage in your life.

The key is learning how to let go, and this is of course very difficult to master but with sound practices to follow and discipline you can defeat the monster within and claim back control of your life.

This is the battle between the dark and the light and coming to the realisation that this all takes place within you is truly a momentous step on your spiritual journey.

# Chapter 5

*'Many of the things that are pushed upon the masses creates negative emotional molecules, once they are formed they are real and you can't get them out of your body unless you know how'.*

**-Don Tolman**
Whole Foods Nutritionist and Author

## Removing trapped emotions

I am going to give you four excellent practices to follow that will help you release your inner negativity (inner gremlin) and at the end of the book you will find references to other techniques and books, which you can research yourself.

In fact just Google 'removing trapped emotions' and plenty of good information will come up. It's well worth trying different methods to find what suits you best. Often what works well for one person may not be suitable for another so trying them all is the best way to decide.

The four methods I recommend are called 'Happy Thoughts' (ideal for children), 'Visualising Your Inner Lake', 'The Notebook Method' and 'Inner Peace Meditation'.

And the purpose of these techniques is to train yourself to focus on something positive and serene at all times, especially when your ball of inner negativity sparks into life.

Essentially you are training yourself to respond to whatever life throws up rather that react. This is the key not reacting, not giving energy or attention to negative dramas or thought patterns that pop up.

You must learn to become the master of your emotions instead of them mastering you.

And the skill you must cultivate to do this is falling into a state of surrender and that means completely accepting whatever is happening without buying into any emotional surges that may be tugging at you, no anger, frustration, annoyance, exasperation etc, you must train yourself to respond rather than react and this will help you to hold your inner peace at all times. Your inner peace is your indicator that you are in the best possible mindset consistent with the state of surrender.

When your inner peace is disturbed you may feel shimmers of energy moving through your body which can then very easily erupt into emotions such as anger, frustration, anxiety, fear etc and this is telling you your gremlin is feeding.

**44**

This is the secret, training yourself to know when the gremlin is active and stirring within you.

You must unlearn what you have thus far been trained to automatically do; you must control your inbuilt instinctive emotional reactions to events when they unfold.

So you settle into your serenity by following the visualisations and hold it as much as possible throughout your day even when you are buffeted by negative energies vying for your attention because as you now know, this is your gremlin waking from its slumber.

This is the key to mastering control and when you do this successfully you will be whittling away at your inner negativity because every time you manage to remain detached from it when it is clawing at you and not react, you release some of it, so it is effectively shrinking.

*"Your task is not to seek for love, but merely to seek and find all the barriers within yourself that you have built against it."*

**-Rumi**
13th century Persian poet

Rumi explains it perfectly, to find love in your life you must remove the gremlin then you will rise up in vibration and come into harmony with love.

As long as the gremlin (the mass of negative slow vibrating sludge) is holding you down in vibration you will find it difficult to feel love because it is just out of reach existing at a higher frequency.

Love is a very high frequency energy that we feel and access when our vibration rises.

# Method 1

## Happy thoughts (ideal for children)

A simple technique for a child is called 'happy thoughts', which basically gives them one easy practice, which you can help them follow. It allows you to keep an eye on them when they feel unhappy or triggered by negative emotions.

In other words when they may feel angry, sad, upset, stressed, irritated, anxious, scared, naughty, belligerent, hyperactive, fidgety, lacking focus, depressed, apprehensive etc.

Or what I refer to as distracted or disturbed due to the influence of their inner gremlin.

How it works is, first you establish a happy memory that they can go to in their mind, which you can spend some time discussing and creating with them. This is their sanctuary, their go to place, that they can think of when needed. I suppose you could see it as an imaginary comfort blanket.

Spend some time talking this through with them so they really take it on board and explain that this is their special place where they can feel safe, protected and happy.

It could be based on an actual favourite place they have been to, maybe on holiday or even just their bedroom where they feel safe and secure, or it could even be thinking of someone close to them that gives them comfort and makes them feel loved, anything they have happy memories of or feel good thinking about.

Once you have settled on the memory tell them a little story built around it, in which you can also introduce key trigger points, such as they were on holiday playing in the swimming pool and a <u>red balloon</u> suddenly appeared and they had great fun laughing and giggling as they passed and chased the balloon around the pool.

This reference to the <u>red</u> <u>balloon</u> whether it actually happened or not, (you can make some of it up), can become the trigger word that you agree with them, that you can say when you may feel they are in a negative mindset or when they are having a negative reaction to something.

So from then on you just say '<u>red</u> <u>balloon</u>' when needed and encourage them when they hear this to take a few deep breaths and on the out breath release the negativity that is trying to engage them.

They could imagine it whooshing out of the top of their head like a kettle letting off steam.

**48**

You can make up any trigger words that suit depending on the memory such as 'fun', 'sunshine', 'football' etc just an agreed word or phrase that you tell them takes them instantaneously back to their happy safe place and remember to emphasise when they are there how safe they are and how good they feel.

Just explain to them that when you say the trigger word they will instantly feel better because it will put a picture in their mind of their happy place and remind them of the nice feelings they have when they think of this place, which immediately allows any negative feelings to fall away. The few deep breaths will help them to shift focus and picture the negative energy being released.

You can then say the trigger word when required such as when they are reacting negatively to something rather than calmly dealing with it. And this will give you a role in helping train their mind to not buy into negative energy when it pops up.

This works because you are interrupting the negative energy charge when it surges through them in whatever form it takes such as anger, jealousy, frustration etc, and this momentary interruption is enough to break the momentum of the energy lessening its negative impact. Even if you think it's not working keep doing it and

*'A new simple solution'*

soon you will see results it's important to stick with it. So this helps them develop an instinctive way of efficiently processing negative surges, instead of the old way of fully buying into them and taking on board maximum damage, whilst fully recharging the said energy in the process. Just keep up the monitoring and reminding them what it means and you will really help them develop an automatic positive attitude trip switch, to lives niggles. And remember it's all about breaking the momentum when the negativity is active. This is all you need to do, this is the practice and it will pay off a thousand fold literally for the rest of their life.

If your child struggles with following this method don't worry because there is still something you can do. And that is keep trying yourself to practice the discipline of not reacting, this will still pay dividends because you will be controlling the energy environment in a positive way. Rather than stoking the fire so to speak, when you readily and emotionally engage with negativity every time it arises.

Anything you can do to maintain a calm serene family home will help anyone in that home who may be suffering with or potentially suffering with mental health problems. A peaceful environment is far more beneficial than a toxic environment, its a higher vibration and generally speaking mental health problems or the

**50**

risk of will lessen the higher the vibration you exist in. Following a practice of non reaction should be followed by anyone looking to improve their lives and as a byproduct the lives of others they are in close contact with.

*'Non reactive behaviour is not a denial of emotions, but rather a release from the reactive patterns that bind us'.*

### -Knowledge Words

An example of how to apply the method:

Maybe they have a pet let's say a dog that they love very much and when they think of their pet this could put a smile on their face and flood them with nice feelings. So you could establish a little story of when they had fun with the dog such as playing in the garden or throwing a ball for the dog at the beach and allow them to relive the fun and happiness this generated.

Your trigger word could then be the name of the dog such as one particular lovely little dog I do know who brings lots of love and joy to his family called 'Bear'. So every time you see them drawn into negative thoughts and actions you would just say 'Bear' to them and with repetitive practice this will jolt them back to a better feeling place. And in time it will become instinctive to detach from any negative thoughts or situations as soon as the trigger word is said, training is the key.

This works amazingly well just try it and see and remember the more you practice this the more habitual and normal it becomes for them to instantly switch from negative to positive feelings.

The benefit of this practice is that while you are training the child to let go of negativity and shift into a more positive mindset, you will not only be slowly breaking down and releasing their inner gremlin but also be able to see clearly just how much of a problem they have.

You can even keep a check on how many times per day you have to say the trigger word and then compare it to say a month from now. This way you can gauge their progress.

And remember every time you say the trigger word you are helping your child or the child in your care have a better future, a future where they understand the importance of not reacting to negativity, which in turn decreases the future possibilities of developing mental health issues.

# Method 2

## Visualising Your Inner Lake

Picture a beautiful turquoise blue lake inside your chest; imagine for the moment the surface of the water is slightly disturbed; this is caused by waves of negative energy pulsing outwards from your ever active inner ball of negativity.

(Rumblings from your inner gremlin)

This creates a rippling across the surface which intensifies when something stressful occurs or when your thoughts drift more towards the negative, or even when somebody brings negative energy into your immediate surroundings through their mood and presence.

Now I want you to take a few slow deep breaths and see the water becoming perfectly still not a ripple upon the surface just a flicker of glistening sunlight bouncing off the now calm and perfectly still lake. Hold that beautiful image and continue taking slow deep breaths.

As you gently focus on your breathing I want you to feel the stillness this beautiful image evokes within you, sense the tranquility and let it wash over you.

This is your inner peace and serenity that you are now picturing and feeling; bask in this moment for twenty to thirty seconds as you focus on your breathing.

During your day remember to occasionally take a deep breath especially if you sense inner turmoil stirring to bring you instantly back to the calm still lake.

This will hone your skill at detaching from any negativity when it arises. keep practicing going back to the stillness and you will soon master this little exercise.

This is what you must learn, initially calming the waters and then holding the picture of the calm still lake within and the feeling of serenity it generates, no matter what is happening on the outside.

I often relax close my eyes and imagine I am visiting my lake, I might see myself sitting on a deck chair at the waters edge for a while watching the ebb and flow of the water or maybe drifting in a rowing boat on the still waters enjoying the peace and tranquility.

The more you practice this type of visualisation the better you will get at doing it and it will become instinctive to hold yourself in a state of inner peace rather than being constantly engaged by the never ending stream of turbulence.

Before long you will be able to walk through your day undisturbed by all the never ending mayhem that takes place around you because you will be able to take refuge and bask in the peace and serenity generated by the image of your inner lake.

You will have trained yourself to settle into the eye of the storm and the sense of inner peace this generates will be gently bubbling up from inside of you.

Mastering the mindset of serenity whilst walking in the never ending chaos will help you to release your inner ball of negativity because each time you manage to hold your inner peace and not become angry, irritated, stressed, worried, frustrated, anxious etc you will be breaking it down and letting some of it go.

Every time you manage to not get drawn in by your gremlin you release some of its energy and it becomes slightly weaker.

This is a spiritual practice and something that you should always be trying to incorporate into your thought process because when you focus on this image and the associated feelings your vibration will rise and that means whatever you are doing in your regular everyday life will improve.

**55**

This is because you have lifted up your vibration and are holding it there while you go about your everyday tasks and this will ensure better results for you.

This is what is often referred to as 'getting into the zone' and many sports professionals follow practices like this to hold their vibration up because this allows them to achieve peak performance. It does not stop you going about your daily business and doing what you have to do but it does quieten your normally ever chattering conscious mind and this is a much better mindset to be in than a head swirling with negative thoughts and feelings, which is what most people are habitually experiencing.

Just look around at peoples faces and more often than not they look distracted with a slight frown or faint look of unhappiness and concern on their face and this state of mind has become 'the norm'.

What you can see is an active ball of inner negativity (gremlin) ticking away on auto pilot perpetually gnawing away at them through their thoughts and feelings. As you progress and become more adept at this practice you will notice you become less and less involved in arguments and disagreements.

It's as if you no longer feel the need to be right or to win because you are more focused on holding the feeling of detachment from potential negative feelings rather than proving someone else wrong, regardless of whether they are or not.

It doesn't matter any more and you embody this state of mind, the peaceful serenity that this evokes overrides whatever happens in the emotional tussles taking place. You can still have robust discussions but they are now devoid of the negative emotional charge that previously dominated viewpoints and opinions.

And after a while you will see these episodes become less and less in your life and this is when you will ponder the utter futility of getting into an emotionally charged disagreement with somebody as you naturally gravitate to an altogether higher perspective. A view point from above the ego level so to speak, a higher perspective where your thoughts and words are not tainted by the need to be right.

And this is when you will also realise its not really about forgiving somebody who you feel may have wronged you but more an absolute letting go of the energy charge surrounding the whole situation.

---

Stepping aside from the emotionally charged energy is the key and pivotal in achieving this is not allowing yourself to be drawn into any kind of judgment or need to be right.

'It doesn't't matter' is the mantra and this detached approach is the secret mind hack to releasing the remaining residue of trapped emotions that you still carry.

Forgiving somebody generally means you are still holding onto the belief that they have done something wrong to you, this is you still buying into the energy charge at some level, when completely letting go of that energy charge is what's needed.

So it's not so much forgiveness in terms of another person, it's more letting go of the bad feelings that allows you to release the trapped emotions.

'Let them keep their pain' is the way forward and this approach allows you to break free. This is the key to you taking back control from your inner negativity (gremlin) that has up until this point had a free reign in respect of the powerful influence it has exerted over you.

And this will allow you to move up in vibration, which is the secret to really changing your life.

As Lao Tzu so eloquently puts it releasing your trapped negative emotions is the greatest gift you can give to the world because this changes you into a higher vibrational person and then you automatically help others by the being you have become.

Or to put it another way you help others by the energy vibration that you now exist at because just being in your company will give them an energy boost.

A quick buzz as they hitch a lift up in vibration by simply being in your presence.

This will of course wear off for them as their inner negativity comes back into play but for a brief moment you will have shown them what is possible, you will have enabled them to see how good they can feel.

*'If you want to awaken all of humanity, then awaken all of yourself. If you want to eliminate all of the suffering in the world, then eliminate all that is dark and negative in yourself. Truly, the greatest gift you have to give is that of your own transformation'.*

**-Lao Tzu**
Ancient Chinese philosopher and poet

## Method 3

## The Notebook

This method is easy to incorporate into your day and because it puts you constantly on alert it becomes a spiritual practice that repetitively cleans your mind of negative thoughts, feelings and emotions.

This method is easy to implement and because its 24/7 means you are on a competitive level with your trapped negative emotions, always alert and it will help hold you in the higher vibrations while you work on getting rid of your inner negativity (gremlin).

This means you will see improvements from the moment you start using it.

Now let's have a look at how it works.

When we look at 'inner negativity' through the eyes of high vibrational thinking we can see that someone with not much 'inner negativity' in general exists at a higher vibrational level than somebody with a lot of 'inner negativity'.

They have less of a heavy weight dragging them down (in other words a weaker less powerful gremlin).

**60**

And as you know training yourself not to react when negativity try's to grasp your mind is how you weaken and get rid of your 'inner negativity'.

The following method is called 'The Notebook' and it is very effective at achieving this.

The method:

Get yourself a small notebook and write down every time that you notice yourself feeling negative (angry, frustrated, worried, tense, scared, depressed, anxious, jealous, envious, hateful, hurt, upset, irritated, annoyed, depressed, unhappy, stressed, unloved etc).

Carry your notebook with you at all times and keep an eye on how you feel, so that you can notice when you are feeling negative.

It may be a nasty comment from somebody, you feeling stressed out from losing your key, a twinge of jealousy, an argument with someone, feeling down because you have no money, maybe listening to somebody's problems, or even just your own negative thoughts ticking over making you feel not so good.

Whatever it is, write it down.

**Entries may look something like this:**

*So and so said something nasty about me, I feel **down**.*

*Had a fight with my friend, I am **upset**.*

*I have no money, I feel **stressed and worried**.*

*Somebody stole something from me, I am **angry**.*

*Lost my keys, I am **frustrated**.*

*So and so has been moaning on about their problems, I feel **depressed**.*

It may even be just the way you are feeling with no particular obvious thoughts fuelling it.

I could go on all day as you can see there are endless little niggles that pop up all of the time and most of the time we allow ourselves to feel some form of negativity, we just do it automatically.

This is what you are trying to stop.

It's this daily engaging in negative thoughts and feelings that is keeping the negative energy within you strong.

You are topping up its battery all of the time, you are constantly recharging your 'inner negativity'; you are forever feeding your inner gremlin.

Stop the automatic reactions and your 'inner negativity' will start losing its power and eventually fizzle away. It's the strong emotional reactions like 'outbursts of anger' that give it a powerful super charge and your endless negative thoughts and feelings triggered by the inevitable daily niggles that you encounter that give it a constant trickle charge.

If you didn't allow yourself to feel bad when the daily niggles are happening your 'inner gremlin' would weaken and your energy vibration would rise.

By noticing your thoughts, feelings and emotions you are stopping it in its tracks and this will begin to weaken the negative energy within you. Over time you will start feeling better and better as you slowly rise in vibration.

You are releasing your 'inner gremlin' and cleansing your energy field; and all you have to do is train yourself to write in your notebook.

If you do this everything in your life will improve, you see the higher your vibration the better everything is.

You will soon be vibrating at the vibrational levels where the better stuff is.

Happiness, fun, joy, laughter, kindness, success and love don't exist at the lower vibrational levels you can only feel or experience them when your vibration rises.

So you will be happier more of the time, you will exist where the good stuff is more of the time.

Just like you can't be depressed when you are feeling happy, the two cannot exist together. And again you will find that when you get your vibration up everything works out better and your problems seem to disappear.

You get on better with everybody, have more friends, feel much better and are a lot more successful in whatever you are doing; life just has a habit of working out for the better.

It is possible when you use the 'Notebook' you may find that you have the occasional bad dream.

Where you wake up feeling frightened, stressed, and angry or whatever, this is your 'inner gremlin' trying to get its charge during your sleep.

It happens because you have slowed down its charge during the day by following the Notebook and it is losing the inner battle.

This should be regarded as a good sign that you are on the right track. Treat the bad feelings in your dream exactly the same as during your day, detach from them and write them down.

This is an easy method to follow and it gets the job done. It trains you to observe your thoughts and feelings and recognise when they are negative, which automatically disengages you from the damaging energy.

And that's the secret, not allowing negativity to take you over and live through you.

It is absolutely essential if you want to change your life in a positive that you follow a strategy like this to rid yourself of the inner gremlin within you that is dragging you down.

*'Learn to let go that is the key to happiness'*

**-Buddha-**

## Method 4

## Inner Peace Meditation

Goal is to attain a state of non resistance, non judgment and complete acceptance of what is. In other words a total state of inner peace.

And to learn how to bring yourself back to that state when required, which is basically anytime you may notice you have drifted out of it.

The reason for mastering this skill is the more you can hold yourself in a state of serenity and inner peace, the less infected you will be by the influence of your trapped negative emotions.

And also because you are not recharging the said emotions through identification with them, this will help to weaken and deplete their presence within you.

Also the less you will be drawn into familiar negative circumstances on the outside, that serve only to feed your inner gremlin.

As well as putting you in a more positive vibration beneficial to your mental health.

One of the best ways to become familiar with the feeling of inner peace is walking in nature and taking deep breath's while allowing the essence of nature's natural way of being to wash over you.

This will familiarise you with the feelings of just being. Another way of describing this would be nature teaches you how inner peace feels and this gives you a reference point to align with, a feeling place to tune into. Observe the trees and flowers and see how they have no resistance to what is.

You can literally feel the calm peaceful energy they emanate if you stop and soak it up for a while.

If the wind blows gently or even of storm proportions the trees are in a natural state of completely accepting this intrusion and the leaves flutter gently or are severely lashed without any change or complaint from the tree. So the actual inner peace or tranquility of the tree suffers no disturbance. It is strong and steadfast no matter what is taking place on the outside.

This natural state of complete acceptance is what you should practice trying to attain and hold as you go through everyday of your life. And when you do that, just like the tree you will master holding your inner peace.

You must have an inner feeling of non resistance and serenity just like the tree.

Non resistant meaning you will not allow your inner peace to be disturbed by outside forces; you are focused above all else on holding the feeling of inner serenity.

The tree just is, and no matter what comes along outside of it, wind, rain, snow, storms, birds, searing sunlight etc, the tree's calm peaceful inner state stays the same.

It is naturally in a state of non resistance, and from this state everything that comes its way is simply accepted.

Of course the tree has no option but to accept things but we can still learn from this because even though we can and often do choose to fight and struggle against whatever is going on outside of us, the tree is showing us the best way to handle things and that is not struggling and fighting against outside things.

Serenity and inner peace is our natural state just like a tree but we lose sight of this because of the constant noise that our conscious mind makes tussling with this and battling with that, which is largely due to the influence of the inner negativity we carry.

**68**

We seem to be forever struggling with whatever life throws up.

Being like the tree is the secret, allowing the noise to continue but no longer buying emotionally into it.

Instead prioritise the feeling of inner peace while detaching from but allowing the constant static to rumble on. Becoming the detached observer is the secret rather than being thrown around like a rag doll by whatever comes our way.

So basically you are turning things around, instead of the noise taking centre stage constantly occupying your mind with your inner peace and serenity lost somewhere in the background you bring your inner peace into your main focus and let the static slip into the background.

This is what you should be practicing trying to achieve because the more non resistant you can become to life's events and niggles, the more you will be holding yourself in a higher vibration and naturally processing and releasing your trapped emotional energy.

By simply not reacting to whatever is happening in a negative emotional way, you will be letting go of some of the residue of past traumas trapped in your body.

**69**

When you do react such as get angry, frustrated, worried, stressed, anxious, irritated, disturbed etc, you add to or at the very least solidify even further your trapped emotional energy.

It's all about allowing the inner peace to bubble up inside of you (be like the tree totally at peace and hold this state as much as possible) no matter what you have to deal with on the outside.

This is how you take on less negative energy as you move through life and instead are able to release some of the trapped negative energy as you go along.

You should see every 'problem' as an opportunity instead of it being a problem, it's your response that determines whether it benefits you or damages you.

It's your chance to raise your vibration and change your life for the better, including improving any mental health issues you may have.

If you are suffering from a mental health problem remember it will be more severe the further down the vibrations you are, so increasing your vibration is paramount in helping you overcome any mental health issues.

Gently responding to life from a state of inner peace is the way forward no matter what comes into your experience.

And the more powerful and emotional the experience, the more trapped negative energy you will release or if handled incorrectly take on board.

Here is a short simple meditation you can teach yourself to use to bring yourself back to inner peace whenever needed.

I want this to be short and simple so you can use it anytime and anywhere, so this little exercise should take you no more than 5 minutes, of course it's up to you if you want to stay with it longer.

Start with ten deep breaths what is called square breathing.

• Breath in deeply for 4 seconds
• Hold for 4 seconds
• Breath out slowly for 4 seconds
• Hold for 4 seconds

Repeat cycle nine more times.

Now you are in a calm relaxed state imagine you are a massive strong oak tree, see your roots reaching deep into the earth. In fact your roots are twice as big as what is above the surface, this is how powerfully rooted to the earth you are.

Your branches are thicker below ground than above. Feel the wind blowing your leaves and enjoy the view from the top of your branches across the distant corn fields, you can see in the distance a bright red tractor chugging down the country lane. Even though the wind blows strongly you are such a mighty tree and your connection with the earth is so deep and solid, nothing that happens can possibly disturb your inner peace and complete serenity.

You smile at the winds feeble attempts to get your attention and you rest in total serenity and confidence in your own mighty presence. You judge nothing, resist nothing and rest in absolute acceptance of whatever comes your way. Your feel this as an overwhelming sense of inner peace.

Enjoy being the oak tree for as long as you want; really try to embody the feelings of its strength and majesty. Soak up the peace and serenity this invokes and familiarise yourself with how this feels.

This is how you should be and trying to feel as you go about your daily business.

Remember holding your inner peace when outside energies trigger your emotions is the key to changing your life and improving your mental health.

---

**72**

You can use this simple meditation anytime you have 5 mins spare or anytime you feel the need to settle things down.

This can be your little quick fix go to mediation anytime you need to get back to your inner peace, get used to using it and you will be amazed at the benefits.

I have derived an even quicker fix from this mini mediation to virtually instantly get back to inner peace.

All I do is take a few deep breaths while repeating the following mantra 'I judge nothing and nobody, I have no resistance, I completely accept what is'.

And while I am repeating this a few times I 'feel' my way back to my inner peace, I allow it to bubble up and I have found the more I use this the easier it gets.

And I can do this in a minute or so. I find this really beneficial when buffeted by outside energies.

It's a great way to virtually instantly let go of any outside forces that may be trying to trigger an emotional response from you.

# Chapter 6

## An example (of how your vibration influences your life)

I will give you an example of how influential your early years are in terms of creating your inner gremlin and how it then affects the rest of your life.

This is a typical scenario that I am sure many of us can identify with to some degree.

I will take you through two different life paths that Geoff could have taken depending on the amount of negativity he was subject to in his formative years.

In the first example Geoff is subject to quite a lot of negativity as his parents both carried strong powerful inner gremlins and this meant Geoff would often be in the middle of, or on the receiving end of negative outbursts.

In the second example Geoff was brought up in a much more positive environment surrounded by lots of high vibrational energies where his parents carried much milder inner gremlins.

These examples will show you more or less how it works, of course every individual responds differently and would be affected differently with personality, temperament, sensitivity and genes etc playing a part but this will show you the mechanics of the process.

And remember this is something that we all go through so try to see the similarities to your own experience and bear in mind we all react differently to what we experience.

## Scenario 1

Geoff was brought up in a typical working class household. The family was never well off but they always got by, you could say life was a bit of a struggle.

There were often arguments and when Geoff was young he was subject to all kinds of negative energy generated by his parents.

Anger, frustration, worry, stress, anxiety, unhappiness and fear were common everyday feelings and emotions bouncing around the household.

This negativity took its toll and Geoff picked up many of these energies, which were to stay with him for life.

Sure enough at a very early age he started to show tendencies to be angry, frustrated and unhappy, as the negative energies he had taken on board manifested through him.

'Look at our Geoff' they would say 'a temper on him just like his dad', as if that were something to be proud of and obviously not realising that it was a burden that he would have to carry throughout his life.

A temper that would manifest through him by way of mild irritability, angry outbursts or occasionally even more severe bouts of intense rage or even violence.

This brooding negativity within Geoff kept him firmly rooted to the lower vibrations as it fed mercilessly off his thoughts, feelings and emotions. The gremlin within him was becoming firmly established.

He seemed to be generally in a bad mood or distant somehow, as his inner attention was generally distracted by negative thoughts and feelings.

His inner gremlin was strong within him and you could always sense its presence hovering just beneath the surface.

This played havoc with Geoff's life from day one and he didn't do very well at school even though he was above average intelligence, he just couldn't seem to apply himself and the teachers said he lacked concentration.

In other words he was distracted by what was going on in his mind, the constant thought patterns playing over and over generally of a negative nature due to his strong inner gremlin.

This is how it messes with your mind pushing in thoughts designed to get you worrying about this or that or maybe feeling sorry for yourself.

Its overbearing presence can be relentless in its quest to keep you in a negative state of mind.

Geoff was also a promising footballer but again he seemed to lack motivation and just couldn't be bothered to put the training in needed to advance his chances.

He left school with no qualifications and started hanging around with the wrong types, which occasionally resulted in brushes with the police.

This resulted in a criminal record and as a result poor job prospects. Geoff did eventually get a job at the local Steel Works thanks to his dad's cousin but this didn't work out, as Geoff felt they had it in for him from the start.

After six months he walked out after an argument with the foreman and found himself back as one of the unemployed.

Eventually Geoff got married to Tracy his childhood sweetheart and they had two children.

The marriage was a rocky one from the start with Geoff's temper often causing problems and within three years they were divorced and he found himself in a custody battle to see the children.

This went on for a number of years and created a bitter feud between him and Tracy, as they tussled to and fro over money issues and access. I wish I could say things got better but they didn't and Geoff's life went from bad to worse with him eventually becoming dependant on alcohol and wasting any money that he did have everyday at the pub.

This contributed to problems with his health and at forty-five years of age he found himself with serious health issues.

Geoff's life is typical of many that face a similar difficult and negative childhood. They can never gain control from their inner gremlin that basically devours them in its never ending need for more and more negative energy.

They spend their life at the mercy of their gremlin feeding its needs and destroying their life in the process, they are in fact simply generators of negative energy through their thoughts, feelings and emotions for the demon within. It may help at this point to see your inner gremlin as an intelligent life form in its own right that cleverly plots and manipulates you to get what it wants.

It pushes thoughts into your mind that you think are yours to steer you down the pathways that it wants, which is always ultimately to create more negativity. This is the inner battle of good against evil, the light against the dark, which is taking place within every one of us. It was the voice in Geoff's head that convinced him and drained him of energy so that he couldn't be bothered to go to football training when he was young, you see if Geoff had succeeded at football that would have generated all the wrong types of energy for his inner gremlin, which of course had already established itself within him due to the energy environment he had been subject to from an early age.

---

*'A new simple solution'*

Joy, fulfillment, success and happiness are no good whatsoever to your gremlin it needs much more negative thoughts and feelings from you.

Your gremlin will systematically destroy your chances of success in any direction in order to keep you as a slave to its needs; it doesn't care about you one bit. Many people are even driven to suicide by their inner gremlins.

Geoff's inner negativity went on to sabotage his job, it was the voice in his head telling him that they all had it in for him, which steered him into believing it was him against them.

Then it destroyed his marriage and encouraged the bitter dispute between him and Tracy. Now I am not saying that was all Geoff's fault as Tracy too has her own inner demons, which will also have played their part in the destruction of their relationship.

In truth they were both victims of their gremlins, as their marriage became gremlin against gremlin the basis of many relationships today. Then his gremlin encouraged him onto the drink, which it will convince him is a way of easing the never end stream of negative, thoughts and feelings in other words it will make him feel better.

**80**

Although in fact it just created more through lack of self-worth, guilt and self-hate. Geoff's gremlin was very clever and it spent a lifetime manipulating him to get what it wanted and its biggest weapon was the fact that he didn't know it was there.

This gave it a free reign to quietly and mercilessly go about its destructive business of sabotaging Geoff's life from the inside, while always convincing him somebody else was to blame.

This is what is happening to all of us, maybe to a lesser degree than Geoff or maybe we have it worse than Geoff but we all have it going on.

This is what we are all up against and this is the real struggle of life and its all taking place within our mind.

And our inner demons are getting away with it but not for much longer because their little game is up now that we finally understand what is going on.

## Scenario 2

Now let's have a look at how Geoff's life may have turned out if he had been brought up in a more positive energy environment during his childhood.

---

**81**

Geoff grew up in a working class household in a lovely positive family environment.

Both of his parents carried very little inner negativity and it showed, they were loving, positive and very caring people. They rarely argued and they were in general happy and content.

This positive energy environment meant that Geoff grew up collecting along the way very little inner negativity resulting in him carrying only a mild version of an inner gremlin because in the all important first six years he rarely experienced negativity in the family home nor his immediate environment.

He was shown lots of love by both of his parents and they were both very comfortable telling him they loved him.

All this positive energy in his childhood meant he was living his life in the higher vibrations where negative energy was at a minimum and this gave him confidence in himself.

He knew his parents loved him and he also knew he deserved the best things in life, why shouldn't he after all this was what he was used to.

You could say Geoff was content and happy with himself and grew up with not a lot of negative thoughts and feelings getting in the way. He did really well at school passing all of his exams and he excelled at football captaining the school team.

Geoff really enjoyed his football and couldn't wait for Saturday morning when they had a league game.

When he left school his dad's cousin managed to get him a start at the local Steel Works and Geoff was on his way, within three years he was promoted and he never looked back.

He married his childhood sweetheart Tracy and they had two lovely children.

Geoff's good job meant he could afford one of the big new houses at the end of the road, a new car and an expensive family holiday every year.

They were a happy family and their children also grew up with little inner negativity holding them back. Geoff and Tracy stayed together throughout their lives and now have three lovely grandchildren.

This is exactly how it works, if you grow up in a negative energy environment you will pick up and get stuck with lots of damaging inner negativity that will manifest through you for the rest of your life.

Your inner gremlin will be more powerful and influential in your life making everything more difficult in the process.

If you grow up in a positive energy environment you will pick up very little inner negativity so you will not be carrying inside you something that will wreak so much havoc in your life.

You can see clearly how it works; with a powerful dose of inner negativity Geoff had a difficult struggling life, with a small dose of inner negativity Geoff was free to have a great and much happier life.

The question is which path do you want your children to take because it's up to you?

It's your responsibility to fill your family home with as much high vibrational energy as possible, as much love, joy, fun, positive encouragement and happiness as you can.

Give your kids quality time and keep the negativity out.

*'A new simple solution'*

If you are fortunate enough to carry only a little inner negativity yourself you will be doing this naturally and now you can see exactly how important this is.

If you carry a heavier dose of inner negativity you may be allowing too much negativity in but now you understand how it works so you can do something about it.

And don't forget even though we don't remember most of our first six years we are still left with an energy imprint, a vibrational range that we have basically downloaded through what we have experienced.

And we then become tethered to this frequency range usually for the rest of our lives as the inner negativity we picked up manifests and replenishes itself through us.

Essentially you become a slave to the gremlin within.

The three methods are great ways for you to start breaking down and releasing your inner gremlin so that you can rise in vibration.

It's never too late to change things and the sooner you get started the better.

## The Negative Rut

Just a quick word about being brought up in a more negative environment, a childhood that leaves you with a strong dose of inner negativity (like Geoff in scenario 1) can chain you to a life in the lower vibrations, a life stuck in a negative rut.

This can lead to all sorts of problems and difficulties and many in this position end up unemployed, in poor health, in financial trouble, problems with drugs and alcoholism, relationship issues, depression, in prison etc.

A lethargic attitude to work may develop and even a festering intolerance for authority of any sort plus many other negative traits.

It's not a nice place to spend your life but unfortunately many in this day and age are finding themselves stuck here and it is almost impossible to get out of. It is effectively a trap, a swamp of negative energy that sucks you in during childhood and keeps you down.

Many living in this low vibrational place find that their inner negativity becomes so powerful it is manifesting through them virtually all of the time.

This is a potentially very unhappy place to spend your life.

When lots of people slip into this condition the negative energy that is generated can spiral out and hurt all of us, as the town, county or even country that we live in gets dragged down by this overpowering force.

You only have to look around to see evidence of this happening all around us right now.

It creates more poverty, crime, abuse, vandalism, violence, mental issues and illness of all kinds. The more negative the place or area the more it will look dirty, untidy, scruffy, un-maintained and generally run down.

This is negativity that you are seeing, the negativity in the people's minds that are living there, it's spilling out into the environment. It's not their fault it's just the way that they have been taught to think about the world and themselves.

It's completely different in a place that is populated with more positive minded people, nice gardens, no litter, well maintained pristine properties, etc.

You can even feel the energy is different, nicer and lighter even brighter in some way.

A major change of mindset is required to break people free from the negative rut mentality and we can start with the children in our care by doing all we can to ensure that they have as positive as possible an upbringing, in the best possible energy environment that we can create.

I believe we can turn it all around and we have to start right now with the children in our care.

Getting stuck in a negative rut is virtually guaranteeing a lifetime of unhappiness and problems that will give you a very difficult life path to follow.

Ensuring that we do all we can to keep the negativity out of children's lives and teaching them how it works will empower young people and give them a much more positive outlook and this will help them to avoid slipping into the negative rut mentality and give them a better future, a happier future, which will benefit us all.

*'Your kids don't need a perfect Mum, they need a happy one'*

**-The Parent Bible-**

# Chapter 7

*'Our thoughts can make us sick'*

**-Joe Dispenza**
Neuroscientist, Lecturer and Author

## Conclusion

So practicing the methods will enable you to become more aware of the way you think and feel, as well as teaching you what it feels like to be in the higher vibrations, which is of course a better place to be for your mental health.

This in turn provides a positive anchor point that you can train yourself to quickly return to when negativity rears its ugly head. And the added bonus is that following this practice of detaching from your negative emotions when they flare up, is that this will also release some of those emotions therefore enabling you to naturally start drifting upwards in vibration.

**This is how you 'change yourself' or to put it another way 'love yourself' and loving yourself is how you start the process of creating the life you always wanted.**

You see loving yourself is about getting rid of all the negativity inside of you that keeps you held down in vibration away from love. It's about getting rid of the gremlin within.

As Rumi says you remove all the barriers you have built against love.

It's not about trying to like or appreciate yourself more while you are still carrying lot's of inner negativity because it will always infect and drown out your efforts, it's about removing the negativity (the gremlin) then you will drift up in vibration to a place where you are naturally happier and more appreciative of yourself, others and your life.

Detachment from gremlin influenced negative surges is the key to a higher vibrational existence, an existence naturally filled with more self-love and appreciation in every sense of the word.

The current way that you are managing negativity by essentially giving it free reign in your life and fully engaging it every time it flares up is simply adding to its power and keeping you trapped in the lower vibrations where you will have much more of it to contend with.

You are essentially being held down by your inner gremlin.

You are unknowingly through your programmed instinctive reactions keeping yourself stuck in the quagmire of negativity, which compounds any difficulties or challenges you may have to face.

You are perpetually replenishing the needs of your inner gremlin, whilst neglecting the needs of yourself.

Life has taught us all to behave in this way and it has become the natural and automatic way of responding to life's events but that needs to change.

Now you have the knowledge of what is really taking place it's time to control how you react and get rid of the gremlin within that has up until this point had a free reign.

**And I believe this is the main factor behind the 'mental health crisis' that we are seeing sweeping across the world today.**

Our gremlins have us trapped and we spend most of our time on the perpetual hamster wheel feeding them with our negative emotions, to all intents and purposes we have become a slave to the gremlin within.

---

*'A new simple solution'*

To move away from the majority of mental health problems we just have to work on releasing our trapped negative emotions our gremlin and raise our vibration.

In other words shrinking the gremlin is the way to salvation.

It worth considering that most of the mental health problems we see flaring up in our children, bullying, depression, anxiety, eating disorders, self-harming, self-hate, ADHD etc may well be flaring up because of the trapped emotions that they carry.

I suspect in a great deal of instances this may well be the case, so mental health issues in the majority of cases are in fact symptoms of carrying trapped emotions and being stuck at a lower vibration.

Of course we are all different and respond differently to whatever energies we experience so what may create extreme damage in one child or person may hardly touch another.

Its not anyone's fault that this happens its simply the experience of life but in this day and age of seemingly more sensitive souls the damage often appears worse than that of years gone by, when people were apparently made of sterner stuff and more resilient.

**92**

This is more than likely due to a somewhat harsher upbringing with much less in the way of material comforts, which naturally instilled a form of mental toughness.

Previous generations had it a little harder and with hindsight that may have not been too bad a thing.

Although I am not saying this generation is pampered and soft but the current way things are does not lend itself like it did in the old days to engendering mental toughness.

So unfortunately the current generation is suffering more in mental health terms and they need our help to understand why this is happening to them and be shown how they can overcome this.

# Chapter 8

## Important Points

*'The first six years have so much to do with
how the next 80 turn out'*

**-Bill Gates Snr-**
Co-Chairman of the Bill and Melinda Gates
Foundation

In the following chapters I want to look at
important things that can affect our
mental health as we are growing up with
special emphasis on how children can
suffer damage.

And then a brief look at the most common
mental health problems that young people
suffer from.

During their early years children inevitably
will suffer some emotional damage, which
in some cases eventually turns into mental
health problems then or maybe in later life,
such as bullying, depression, self harming,
eating disorders, ADHA, depression, drug
abuse, alcohol abuse etc.

So firstly let's look at what is at play in
those early years and what can be done to
make things better and lessen the impact
of negative energy.

## The important first six years

Your job as a parent is the most important responsibility of your life.

You are literally (especially in your child's first six years) determining the future that your child will have because whatever you tell them, show them or allow them to be exposed to, they readily and innocently accept.

They are downloading information on a daily basis through what they see and hear happening in front of them and during the first six years they have no filters or previous experience to draw on, so they simply accept whatever happens as absolute fact.

You are teaching them how the world is through your behaviour, actions, beliefs and expectations and they eagerly and unquestioningly download this information into their subconscious mind, they soak it up like a sponge.

Essentially you are loading their hard drive which they will carry and be governed by for the rest of their lives.

This is why it is so important that you do your very best to ensure that they grow up in the best possible energy environment.

The energy imprint that they are left with is generally and vibrationally where they will spend most of their life.

Any negative energy that you express and show them or allow them to be subject to they readily take on board and this begins to form their trapped emotions or inner gremlin.

This early years downloading sets the vibrational levels or comfort zones that they will more than likely be chained to for good and once the boundaries are set, it can be very difficult to break free from them.

As parents you are setting out the blueprint for your child's future, you are determining vibrationally where they will spend the rest of their lives.

You are having a massive influence on whether they have a life of struggle and strife or success and happiness depending on what you teach and subject them to, especially in the first six years, just like Geoff in scenario one and two.

It's all about the energy that you allow into your family home and your job is now that you are aware to bring them up in a home filled with as much high vibrational energy as possible.

A home filled with love, happiness, joy, kindness, laughter, fun, consideration, caring, unselfishness, encouragement, discipline, sensible rules, good routines, strict sensible bedtimes etc.... is vitally important to how your child will feel about themselves and the world around them for their entire lives.

Sensible rules and discipline shows your child that you care and that you love them, lack of rules and discipline they can very easily subconsciously interpret as maybe you don't love them and don't care so much.

Remember a negative environment leaves the door open ajar for their inner gremlin to grow and go about its business of subtly influencing their thoughts, feelings and beliefs.

It's important here to understand that when as a parent you discipline and teach your children good manners, as well as teach them how to be thoughtful and considerate to others, you are helping them to grow up feeling good about themselves.

This helps dignity, self-respect, pride and unselfishness to develop and flourish all of which encourage positive thoughts and feelings about the self.

And of course when you are nice and kind to other people they are nice and kind to you, they are not having negative thoughts and feelings about you, they are not firing negative energy at you.

If you let children misbehave and get away with it you are in fact by not correcting their behaviour when they are inconsiderate, negative and thoughtless to others, saying it is okay to behave in that way without respect for others.

You are teaching them its okay to act in a selfish negative disrespectful way that doesn't take the feelings of others into account.

This can establish within them habitual negative behaviour patterns, which will damage them in the long run, as they will when displaying selfish behaviour be faced with frustration, anxiety and anger from the people that they are hurting, irritating and annoying. This creates a negative cycle of energy that will as long as they are putting it out there rebound back onto them.

Antagonising, irritating, disrespectful, belligerent and spoilt behaviour creates frustration, anger, annoyance, exasperation and bad feelings coming back at them and this just strengthens or even adds to the inner negativity within them.

**98**

This cements them even more firmly to the vibrational level they are at adding strength and power to the gremlin within.

Remember the energy environment that you grow up in generally becomes the energy environment that you spend the rest of your life in.

A childhood full of anger, hate, struggle, frustration, disillusionment and the experience of parents that don't bother to administer discipline correctly because they don't understand the consequences or are too selfish to care, condemns your child to a life surrounded by thoughts, feelings and emotions that embody these types of energies, which means they will attract experiences that reflect these types of energies.

They can end up stuck for a lifetime in repetitive negative energy cycles of their own making as their inner gremlin continuously replenishes itself at their expense.

If they make other people feel negative in any way through their behaviour and lack of consideration you need to correct the behaviour and explain to them it's not acceptable to treat anybody in this way. And if they do treat people badly they will be treat like this by others.

If you don't then you are allowing bad traits to develop which can soon become entrenched within their personality and this is always going to come back and hurt them.

Its simple put good energy out get good energy back, put bad energy out get bad energy back. Follow this simple guideline and you will be getting it right and this is good parenting and of course most parents understand and naturally do this.

On the other hand a childhood full of love, compassion, kindness, happiness, joy, fun and real thoughtful caring parenting means a lifetime surrounded by these types of energies attracting these types of experiences.

Like Geoff in scenario two.

I am sure I know where I would prefer my children to be. You are determining the level and strength of 'inner negativity' that your child will have through your positive influence and behaviour in front of them.

The importance of this cannot be underestimated.

Quality time spent playing with your child will help them much more than simply telling them to watch a DVD or entertain themselves with a computer game.

**100**

Of course there is nothing wrong with computer games (some of them) or DVD's especially when you encourage them with love and affection to enjoy watching or playing but when it's done with frustration and stress because you can't be bothered you are creating the wrong energy.

Really it's about getting the balance right and when you have got time for them always try to be positive, interested and loving, as this affirms your love for them.

Try to keep negative energy out of your home, never argue in front of the children.

If you have a disagreement sort it out when the kids are not there. Never let them hear about any problems that you may be having.

Every family will experience the everyday ups and downs of life, arguments, money issues, health problems, cars breaking down, boilers bursting, washers flooding the kitchen etc.

When these things happen accept them without the negativity that is usually generated, keep the frustration, anger, stress, worry, anxiety etc, out of it especially in front of the children.

It's important that you do your best to manage your mind and stay positive in all types of situations.

Any negative energy that gets into your family home will have a negative impact on your children **for life**.

Many TV programmes are even filled with negativity.

Even the soaps are now massive generators of negative energy. Subjecting your children and indeed yourself to negative energy from your TV set is not good for either of you and if your children are under six years old the damage can be long lasting.

There are positive options, feel good movies; cartoons, fun game shows and comedies are a much better form of entertainment to allow into your home than programmes filled with anger, arguments, frustration and even violence.

Be positive about money, health and relationships.

Your relationship with money is what they download and become stuck with. If you struggle with money or always have the feeling of never having enough, they will likely pick this up and absorb this energy from you.

They will then be monitored by their inner gremlin for the rest of their lives to always feel that money is a struggle.

For example years later when they get the chance of a good, well-paid job they may find that they are driven from within to find someway to sabotage that opportunity.

They will fail because their inner gremlin wants them to because it is sticking to the energy boundaries downloaded in childhood.

I have seen people do this (and done it myself) time and time again, come up with a list of feeble excuses to leave a good job, often it defies logic and it's never their fault there is always somebody else to blame.

It's never them but in fact it is always them, it's their inner gremlin getting its way and keeping them in the vibrational comfort zones that suit its damaging agenda.

What you are witnessing is the person's gremlin talking them into it, it has a different goal and it's not always in their interests, it simply wants to stick to the vibrational boundaries because this ensures its survival, this keeps the negative energy flowing.

**103**

It wants to keep the negative energy flowing through their thoughts, feelings and emotions.

This is the routine that keeps it strong and powerful. This is how it survives; it needs negativity on a daily basis to maintain it's presence at the vibrational level it has become used to.

This is how it works; your children absorb your vibrational energy about everything, which forms the gremlin within them.

So be very careful what you subject them to.

Even if you are struggling with money don't show this to them, give the impression that everything is fine and this will help them download a better feeling towards money then they will find years later that money comes into their life more easily.

Typical common negative phrases around the subject of money like 'who do you think I am Rockefeller' and 'money doesn't grow on trees' should never be used in front of your children. This is how you program them negatively about money and when they do get the chance of that well paid job later in life they may find their gremlin getting in the way trying to sabotage their success.

**104**

Unintentional negative programming is the biggest disservice you can do to your children as they are growing up. And of course many parents don't realise they are contributing to this, but now you understand how it works its up to you to change things.

This is why we say love in childhood means a happier more successful life, it really does and I mean love in the broader sense, joy, fun, consideration, thoughtfulness, laughter, happiness, sincerity etc.

Another way of saying it would be 'a childhood filled with high vibrational energies means a better life'.

This applies equally to relationships; your children will observe your relationship and begin forming their inner negativity and beliefs about relationships based on this, which will determine how their relationships will more then likely go in the future.

If they see you arguing they will absorb that energy and it will more than likely manifest in their relationships in the future. If they see you constantly complaining about your health they will more than likely accept that this is how it is and eventually begin doing the same?

**105**

The way that your inner negativity manifests through you programs your children to do the same.

If you want a better life for your children then you must overcome the urges of your inner gremlin and only allow high vibrational energies to enter the family home.

**Always tell your children that they are the best, they can do anything if they try, and they are wonderful, beautiful, amazing, fantastic, incredible, and most importantly that they are loved.**

**You can never tell them this enough.**

**Knowing that your parents love you is the most important factor in keeping their level of inner negativity at a minimum.**

As soon as they are born whisper this (or something like it) to them every night when you put them to bed and you will be programming their subconscious for a successful, happy, high vibrational life:

**'You are beautiful, you are amazing, you can do anything and I love you more than anything in the world'.**

It's all common sense really and now you understand the principles of 'High vibrational thinking' and how you develop your inner gremlin, you can see why allowing negative energy a free reign in your family home can be so damaging.

When they start school and bring you home their school report always talk excitedly about the good points make a big fuss of this, heap the praise on them.

And when that's all done you could quietly mention in good energy (genuine concern, understanding, love) the things they might be able to do better in.

This is the way to keep them feeling good and how to help them do better. Never emphasise the negative issues, make light of them and don't generate any bad feelings when talking about them, no anger and frustration.

Remember negative energy has no place in your home if you are to do the best for your children.

Your job is to ensure that your children have the least possible exposure to negative energy and the maximum possible exposure to positive energy.

This will make sure that they grow up with the best vibrational program downloaded into their mind, which means they will settle at a higher vibration and also carry a less powerful inner gremlin.

This will then help them feel good about themselves and life in general, which will create the best possible life path in the future, free from many of the problems and difficulties that we have all been subject to.

Most of us have grown up in an environment where negative energy has run rampant and our parents had no idea that the daily engagements of negativity were damaging us.

Arguments, anger, moaning, stress, anxiety, fear, frustration, negative gossip and lack of affection were considered normal thoughts, feelings and emotions to express. This gave many of us a difficult life path to travel chained to the lower vibrational zones by the weight of our 'inner negativity'. No wonder so many people have struggled in their lives.

Well now you know how it works you have the opportunity to change all of that for your children. It's very simple, the lower your vibration the harder everything is, all the problems exist down there so why would anybody want to live down there.

It's simple stay in the higher vibrations and life is wonderful.

Happiness, success, peace, joy and love exist in the higher vibrations and that's where you want your children to live their lives.

Create a home for them with as much high vibrational energy as possible, this will give them the least possible 'inner negativity' ensuring that they will exist and live their lives at the highest possible vibration and you will have achieved the greatest success of your life.

### Remember the first six years are the most important.

A strong and powerful level of 'inner negativity' means a life of struggle and the more of it there is the worse it will be.

A low level of 'inner negativity' means a far easier, happier and more successful life in the higher vibrations where all the good stuff is.

The best thing you can do now for your children is work on breaking down and releasing your inner negativity. This will make it easier for you to keep negative energy out of your home and this will ensure a better energy environment for your children.

So practicing one of the methods will pay big dividends for you and your family.

*'Parents if you let your child argue with you, they will argue with me.*

*If you let your child speak to you in a disrespectful tone, they will take that tone with me.*

*If you allow your child to break rules without consequences, they will not do what I say either.*

*You see you are your child's first and most important teacher, we can only build on the foundation you have laid at home.'*

**-Bored Teachers**

# Chapter 9

## Bullying

From an energy point of view it's easy to understand why a bully behaves in a hurtful way to other people, it's because their energy field is often vibrating at a slow rate due to having a lot of inner negativity (trapped emotions) or as I say a powerful inner gremlin.

This holds them most of the time in the lower vibrations where it really doesn't feel very nice, they often feel afraid, unhappy, miserable, uneasy, worthless, anxious, not as good as other people and even depressed. It could be because they are having or have had a difficult unhappy childhood or are facing other problems in their life.

Or maybe they live where lots of people around them are bullies and they have been bullied a lot, so they have become used to the awful feelings associated with bullying and this has programmed them to behave in a bullying way. Whatever the reason they have a desperate need to find some relief from the uncomfortable negative thoughts and feelings that plague their mind and this drives some to fall into a behaviour pattern that is unfortunately focused on dragging down someone else's energy vibration.

---

**111**

They call someone a nasty name; the person attacked feels hurt and upset so they experience a drop in their vibration and this makes them feel unhappy.

The bully feels powerful and strong for a brief moment and this gives them a temporary boost up in vibration and this makes them feel happy.

**A bully is basically stealing your happiness without any concern for how it makes you feel.**

The attack on somebody causes the bully to momentarily engage misguided thoughts and feelings of superiority, strength and power and this is what gives them a quick boost up the vibrations and makes them feel better for a very short while.

They may even engage in laughter and glee which helps boost them up even further as they inflict the suffering, which confirms again that they don't understand how much this hurts the victim.

Bullies only think of themselves and what they want, they have little understanding or consideration for how their victim feels.

After a short while the quick boost wears off and their constant habitual negative thoughts and feelings return (their inner negativity or gremlin takes over again).

This drags their vibration back down to its 'normal' lower level and then it's back to feeling not so good.

This is when the automatic dysfunctional behaviour cycle kicks in again and they are on alert ready to react when the next opportunity to bully and hurt somebody presents itself. Basically they are under the control of their inner gremlin dancing to its tune.

From a HVT point of view they are playing a never ending game of snakes and ladders, up one minute and down the next.

It's really simple, help the bully get rid of their inner gremlin, which is behind all of their negative thoughts and feelings and their vibration will rise naturally.

The rise will be permanent and they will no longer automatically behave in this negative way, they will stop bullying because they will not need to do this to feel better. The habitual behaviour manner in which they have become stuck will no longer be controlling them.

They will not need to keep boosting their vibration up but if they don't do something to release their inner gremlin they will be stuck in this relentless loop of misery.

It's not relevant what form the bullying takes or the reason they use to attack the victim because boosting up their vibration is the only objective and remember that's all happening on autopilot.

Calling someone names, sending a nasty text message, physical violence, homophobic bullying, racist bullying, cyber bullying or whatever is all about achieving the same result, giving the bully a temporary boost in vibration. They have found this makes them feel better and become locked into this dysfunctional cycle of behavior.

They may single out the victim because they have something they don't (lots of money, happy family life, doing well at school, new job etc) or are different to them in some way (different hair colour, skin colour, bigger ears, overweight etc) but this is just so they can use that as an excuse to poke fun or be nasty, which will get them what they really want. The bully doesn't necessarily hate or dislike the person or people that they attack they are just using them.

The only person they really don't like is themselves and this self hate is coming from their inner gremlin the true source of their suffering. And the motivation is always the same, to make themselves feel better at the expense of someone else.

If they can cajole or encourage others to join in and also laugh and poke fun at the victim they feel even better, this gives them a bigger boost up because in a twisted way this makes them feel supported, admired, approved and justified in what they are doing, again all energies and emotions that increase your vibration even if it is only a short term boost.

This daily routine of making other people unhappy to get a brief moment of happiness, a brief boost up is how it works because any relief they can get from their usual negative thoughts and feelings feels better to them.

It's all about a quick boost up the vibrations then after a short while back down again.

They are locked into a repetitive behaviour cycle a real hamster wheel of negativity.

Most bullies probably don't even release they are bullies, they are simply so unhappy most of the time because of the constant strong presence of their inner gremlin that they crave relief and this has pushed them into behaving this way.

*'A new simple solution'*

In the bully's case this behaviour pattern was probably locked into place because they may well have suffered getting bullied themselves or observed bullying or it could be that they have just subconsciously fallen into this method to make themselves feel better but it's the same old answer, it doesn't matter how they got like this, get rid of their inner negativity, the gremlin within and they will stop bullying, they will be cured.

Bullying is a negative behavioural manifestation caused by their inner gremlin holding them down in vibration; it is happening because they desperately want relief from their never ending negative state of mind. Bullying will be more prevalent in environments or neighbourhoods that are in general more negative. So you will see more bullying taking place in the inner cities than out in the countryside because the inner cities are in general lower in vibration.

**Bullies need to be pitied rather than feared because they are manipulated, weak and unhappy**, not strong and powerful.

They are not strong enough to ignore and control their inner gremlin and this causes them to seek relief by hurting others.

Many other people feel the same when plagued by their inner gremlin but are strong enough and thoughtful enough to put up with it without feeling the need to hurt other people so they can feel better.

Bullies are not strong enough to do this and they are too emotionally immature to care or understand how their horrible, unfeeling words and actions cause terrible pain to others.

**Bullying is a weakness, carried out by a weak troubled person.**

They are being overpowered and used by their inner gremlin, which causes them to behave in this negative way and they more than likely have no idea what's going on.

The majority of the time they are sad, unhappy people too mentally weak to resist the urge to lash out at another to ease their pain.

Don't react to a bully's taunts and they will not get the boost in vibration they are after, so the bully will soon leave you alone.

In fact not reacting will backfire on the bully because they will then feel ineffective, less powerful, weak etc and this means they will actually get the bad feelings not you.

**117**

So they will feel worse when you simply smile at them and don't react but the more you react the bigger the boost up for them, so the more likely they will feel drawn to bully you again.

This is why some people get bullied all of the time because the bullies see that they always react, they openly show that they feel hurt, upset, annoyed etc and this makes them more of a target.

When you react and **'feel'** really hurt over a period of time there is a danger that you could slip into a victim mentality and this means you end up almost expecting to get bullied.

You really fear it and this can put you in a nervous, scared, lonely, apprehensive mindset that shows in all of your actions.

You can end up feeling isolated and vulnerable, which could generate even more negative thinking and feeling from your inner gremlin and at worst over time lead to depression, anxiety, self-harming, drug problems etc.

This spiral downwards into the lower vibrations also means you are more than likely going to stand out to bullies and attract them.

This can even make you a target for others who may not normally bully but are encouraged by the bully and you could then suffer collective bullying.

**However don't feel bad if you get bullied, remember the bully is the one that there is something wrong with not you.**

**And nearly everyone has suffered from bullying at sometime in their lives.**

Bullying is an automatic response pattern, a symptom of having a strong and powerful gremlin.

When other people join in and support the bully they are showing their fear, fear that they might also get bullied.

They think if I do it as well the bully will leave me alone but what they are really showing is their weakness, lack of strength and vulnerability.

A strong person would never bully someone else or join in when others are and a really strong person would step in and tell the bully or bullies to leave them alone.

## Magic Mirror

A bullies words and actions can only hurt you if you **'feel'** hurt. This is what they are trying to do, make you **'feel'** hurt. If you think to yourself 'I know the bully is the weak person with the problem and I will not let them make me **'feel'** hurt', then they can't hurt you.

It's the **'feeling'** hurt that they need you to experience for them to get the boost in vibration.

You have to be emotionally triggered for the bully to get what they want so be strong and don't react, don't play their game.

If you refuse to **'feel'** hurt they get nothing from you and they will soon stop attacking you because it won't be working for them.

It only works for them if you allow the feelings of hurt to surge through you. In fact if you can master not reacting as you now know this will make them feel worse and they will after a few attempts of trying to goat you steer well clear of you.

You know they are the one with the real problems, the real bad feelings so let them keep them and train yourself not to react.

Show your inner strength by ignoring their attempts to goad you.

When you really **'feel hurt'** it feels as if they are sucking the energy out of you and inhaling it into them. They are drawing the life force out of you and this leaves you feeling terrible and abused.

You must stop them doing this and you do it by training yourself not to **'feel hurt'**. This will really turn the tables and <u>hurt them</u> this is how you pay bullies back by not reacting.

A good way to teach yourself not to **'feel hurt'** and ignore bullies is the 'magic mirror' exercise and it's very easy to do.

Just imagine a big mirror between you and the bully and when the bully says nasty things to you, texts you or makes negative comments on social media about you etc imagine the nasty words bouncing off the mirror and shooting back at the bully.

Really picture this and you will see the bully's face horrified when their negative energy comes back at them.

The mirror can protect you from them no matter how they are trying to attack you whether you know them or not and remember the more you stay calm and don't react the worse it is for them.

**121**

If you do get attacked take deep breaths and allow this to calm you down then use the magic mirror to see the negativity bounce back to them.

Don't give them the satisfaction of replying verbally or on text etc because this just means you have engaged the negativity.

Just hold your inner peace, smile and let the mirror bounce the negativity back to them.

This works very well just practice it and see you will be amazed at their reaction.

The more you can hold the feeling of knowing you are safe behind the mirror the more it hurts them.

*'A new simple solution'*

# Magic Mirror Exercise

(See the bully's nasty words, text
messages, emails or social media
comments etc bounce off the mirror back
to them)

## If you are getting bullied

Hopefully after reading this book you will have more understanding of what makes one person bully another. You can then practice using the magic mirror method and calm breathing when you need it and also use one of the other methods to start getting rid of your inner gremlin and get your vibration up.

This will soon have you feeling much happier and you will get less attention from bullies. The higher your vibration the less you will attract the attention of bullies. It is always good to talk to somebody if you are getting bullied as this stops you bottling it up which only adds more power to your gremlin.

Bottling it up can make you even more of a target for bullies as your vibration may drop due to the extra negative thoughts and feelings and when your vibration has dropped you may feel more unhappy and nervous about getting bullied, putting you in a more vulnerable position. So just follow the techniques and bullying will soon be a thing of the past **remember if you don't react** the bully gets nothing from you. In fact they get their own nasty negative energy shooting back at them and they get the horrible feelings that they were trying to give you.

# If you are a bully

If after reading this book you recognise that you are a bully you can follow the methods to help get rid of your inner gremlin and this will get your vibration up and this will help you to stop bullying people. In many ways you are also a victim because you are under siege from your inner gremlin which you have acquired through no fault of your own.

Your particular life circumstances have unfortunately left you with the burden of a strong form of inner negativity or trapped emotions and it's this inner negativity that is causing all of your suffering and driving you to act in a bullying way.

It's not your fault that you have fallen into this negative behaviour pattern but it is up to you to do something about it, especially now that you understand how terrible it is for the people that you are hurting.

Remember you will feel much happier if you can leave bullying behind and your life will improve in every way.

Bullying is keeping you stuck in an unhappy place and damaging your life in many other ways.

# **Chapter 10**

## Depression

*'Depression is a low vibrational place that
we all visit at sometime in our lives
unfortunately some people get stuck there'.*

Depression can take endless forms and
there are hundreds of books written about
the causes.

Let's look at it from a HVT viewpoint. When
your energy vibration is dragged down (or
pressed down) deep into the lower
vibrations, which is in most cases due to a
particularly powerful dose of inner
negativity (inner gremlin) and you find it
difficult to function normally we call this
'depression'.

Or possibly you could be experiencing an
unusually active inner gremlin for some
reason; maybe you have gone through
something traumatic like bereavement, a
relationship break up, job loss etc and are
temporarily dragged down further than
your usual vibrational level.

Either way you are in the lower vibrations
and find it difficult to act and behave as
you normally do.

As we know depressed means 'pushed down' and that's exactly what's happened, you have been pushed down the vibrational scale so far, that you have dropped into the very negative lower vibrational zones where negative thoughts and feelings dominate.

There is not much nice stuff down there.

I believe we are all suffering from mild depression to some degree and our inner gremlin is the cause of it.

The more powerful or active our gremlin is the more it drags down our vibration and the more dysfunctional we are likely to be, in other words the more depressed we are likely to be.

Everybody is dysfunctional (because we are all depressed) but we don't classify it as an illness until we really get down to the lower vibrational zones and this is when we seriously begin to malfunction.

This is when we say somebody is suffering from depression; this is when their behaviour becomes labeled and catagorised as a mental illness. The truth is we are all behaving negatively because we are all held down at a lower vibration than our natural state due to our inner gremlin but in general we accept this because it is considered 'normal'.

The people who are behaving even more negatively than what is considered 'normal' we say they are depressed. They are even further down the vibrations than the rest of us and it's very difficult to behave 'normally' down there.

In fact if any of us 'normal' people were further down the vibrations we would also begin behaving like the people we label as depressed and we would also be then classified as suffering from depression.

I sure we all have experienced this at sometime in our lives, its virtually impossible not to experience depression at sometime in our lives.

When you are down there your mind gets so distracted by negative thoughts and feelings that you can't think straight, it's hard to concentrate on simple tasks and you view everything through the eyes of the negative zone that you are chained to.

If you were vibrating at the frequency of love your natural state, you would not be dysfunctional and you could not feel 'depressed'. Often you may believe something is causing your depression such as money troubles, relationship problems, illness, etc, but this is not the case because what is causing you to be 'pressed down' is causing your depression and that is your inner gremlin.

**128**

Your gremlin is dragging you down and encouraging negative thinking and feeling about anything it can and when this is excessive this is what we call depression.

It can affect some people all of the time and others may just experience it occasionally.

I believe people that have bipolar, which is bouts of depression followed by highs are under the powerful influence of their inner gremlin and then released by it when it has had its fill of negative energy.

This releases them from its grasp and they soar up the vibrations only to be dragged down again later when it becomes active again.

Your gremlin will use any subject that it can to promote doom and gloom within your mind to pull you into more and more negative thinking and feeling.

It will blow things totally out of proportion to get you in a state of worry, stress, anxiety, anger, frustration, fear etc, so that it can get what it wants, the negative emotional charge.

It is feeding off your negative feelings.

You are being used to generate its food. It is pushing thoughts into your mind like a little voice in your head telling you how bad everything is or could be.

It may convince you that it is because of money problems, relationship troubles or whatever but the truth is it's your inner gremlin that is orchestrating the whole thing. And the more you think it is your money problems or whatever the more power it has over you, it doesn't want to be found out. If you don't know its there, it can comfortably and easily draw you into states of negativity giving it what it wants.

You are too busy mulling over thought after thought blaming your partner, worrying about your money situation or whatever to see what is really happening. You simply become engulfed by the negative feelings as the thoughts never endingly circulate in your mind. You become a generator of negative energy feeding the monster within.

There really is a very simple answer, get rid of what is dragging you down and you get rid of your depression.

Get rid of your gremlin and you will rise up in vibration and be cured, you will no longer be depressed or 'pressed down'.

Some depressed people also fall into bad habits such as drinking or taking drugs to grasp any rise in vibration that they can manage to ease the suffering, even if it is only temporary.

They will try anything for even the slightest relief, this helps to blot out the painful experience of existing in such a low vibrational negative zone.

Their gremlin has pushed them so far down away from the energy of love that it is often unbearable. Any temporary high gained eases the pain, for a while.

Many alcoholics and drug addicts are locked into this existence trying to escape their inner gremlin, which constantly eats away at them through their never ending negative thoughts and feelings. They don't know how to turn it off, so they numb it with alcohol or drugs.

Get your vibration up and you will feel fine and the horrible feelings of depression would not be able to even enter your mind. Your problems with money or whatever could still be there but it wouldn't feel anywhere near as daunting or important.

Understanding how it works is the first step then you need to take some action to help get yourself back up the vibrations.

Now you have that understanding so the next step is follow the methods and you will soon be on the road to recovery.

Remember the horrible feelings of depression caused by existing in the lower vibrational zones are encouraged by your inner gremlin.

It doesn't care what happens to you, as long as it gets what it wants and that's negative energy from you through your thoughts, feelings and emotions.

It will even push you to complete self-annihilation to get what it wants; this is why many people commit suicide. They take this way out to escape the overbearing relentless attention of their gremlins insatiable appetite for negative energy.

It has no concept of what it is doing to you; it has only one focus more and more negative energy.

It can become a true monster within devouring you from the inside dragging you further and further down in vibration.

If you want to overcome depression once and for all you must follow a method to break down and release your gremlin and you will soon be on your way back up the vibrations to a depression free future.

**132**

# Chapter 11

## Self-harming

This is another way your gremlin can manifest through you and it is almost as if the voice in your head is encouraging you to harm yourself for whatever reason it can dream up such as, do it so people will feel sorry for you or maybe people will care about you or even people will admire you.

Whatever the twisted logic it is not instigated by you because in the majority of cases it is pushed onto you by your gremlin.

It is essentially your inner pain or inner trapped emotions being made manifest.

If you didn't have these trapped emotions inside you, you would not feel the urge to harm yourself.

This is just the way that your inner pain has found to come rushing to the surface, this is the method it has discovered works with you.

And as you now know in someone else it could manifest as bullying, anxiety issues (GAD), depression, drinking, drugs etc.

All of these dysfunctional behaviours come from the same source, your trapped negative emotions, your gremlin within.

And the power and strength of the gremlin determines the severity of the dysfunctional behaviour.

So if self harming is how it expresses itself through you, the stronger the gremlin the more severely you may feel inclined to harm yourself even in extreme cases to the point of suicide.

Don't forget it's not you harming yourself it's your inner gremlin doing it and you just follow orders when it commands you to inflict the damage because you think it's your thoughts prompting you or suggesting it to you.

This is what's really going on, your gremlin is manipulating you, you must wrestle control back from the gremlin.

Unfortunately through the various circumstances that you have had to endure and experience in your life and more than likely through no fault of your own, you have developed a strong inner gremlin and now you are suffering the consequences of that alien presence within you.

As long as you believe there is something wrong with you and you don't realise that you have an inner gremlin that is behind your suffering, it has you caught in the trap.

It can then work quietly and systematically behind the scenes infecting your thoughts and destroying your life.

It operates undetected and free to gorge and replenish itself because every time you harm yourself and then have the corresponding negative thought patterns and feelings that go along with self harming, it feeds off the energy generated.

It's a self perpetuating under the radar process that runs on autopilot, the demon within is using you to satisfy its craving for negative energy.

It is devouring you from the inside keeping you stuck in the lower vibrations which suits its needs best and not yours.

It is holding you down and damaging your life in endless ways, while it goes about maintaining its survival. It has no concept of what is good or bad for you, it just uses you mercilessly for its own self gratification, even if this means in an extreme scenario total destruction of your life in the process.

*'A new simple solution'*

Self harming is a manifestation on the surface of the collective traumas you have suffered in your life.

Release the energy from the traumas that is still trapped inside of you, (the inner gremlin) and the self harming will stop.

In fact it's time we stopped referring to it as 'self harming' because it is actually not something that you do to yourself but 'assault' inflicted upon you by the parasite within.

Maybe it would be more accurate to refer to it as 'parasitic assault'.

# Chapter 12

## GAD

## (Generalised Anxiety Disorder)

Everyone will experience anxiety during their lives, it's probably impossible not to in the world we live in today, it is part and parcel of life, however some people have it more severely and it can disrupt their life in a very negative way. Symptoms of GAD (the more serious version of anxiety which is classified as mental illness when it becomes chronic) are:

Feeling restless, wound up, on edge
Struggling to concentrate
Feeling irritable
Having feelings of worry
Headaches, aching muscles
Other unexplained pains
Sleep problems


Another way to view anxiety is that you are sensing the energy of your inner gremlin.

When your inner gremlin is a powerful negative entity this can persistently manifest all of the extreme symptoms that comprise of the condition that we call GAD.

A strong active gremlin may consistently manifest as anxious feelings and distract you from dealing with your everyday life.

As with other mental health issues working on releasing your inner gremlin will lessen its power over you therefore easing the symptoms of GAD.

So essentially in most cases GAD is caused by having an inner gremlin that has a powerful hold over you.

It is too strong so you need to weaken it by letting go of some of the negative energy that the gremlin is embodying.

Achieving this will lessen the 'symptoms' of GAD. So the symptoms are in fact not the real problem but an indication of the real problem which is your inner gremlin, your collective residue of negative energy left over from the life's traumas you have experienced.

Get rid of the gremlin and you get rid of Generalised Anxiety Disorder.

# Chapter 13

## ADHD

Attention Deficit Hyperactivity Disorder is when a person/child is persistently restless, has difficulty concentrating, is easily distracted, lacks patience, is easily upset and possibly fidgets a lot.

They also may appear to have a short attention span and seem to act impulsively without thinking things through, a sort of hyper reactive behaviour disorder.

This type of behaviour in children is normally evident before they are six years old; the signs are there so to speak. It isn't actually known what causes ADHD but it's thought it could be hereditary.

Possibly years ago when ADHD wasn't a classified mental illness we referred to children behaving like this as 'having ants in their pants' so as with many other now labeled mental illnesses issues it has always been around, we just hadn't put a label on it.

I would suggest in many cases it may well be caused by the presence and rumblings of an unusually active and high energy inner gremlin.

The gremlin for whatever reason is fairly powerful within the person/child and has become a constant source of niggling distraction.

This would draw the attention of the person/child making it difficult for them to go about their normal daily tasks due to their attention largely being preoccupied.

Like when for example you are looking after a distressed baby that is crying and screaming, you would find it difficult to get on with other things due to the distraction, worry and stress created by the situation with the baby.

This distracted mind situation would then create symptoms within the person/child that we associate with the condition. So the gremlin would be an irritating, distracting, confusing type of parasite, which would manifest within the person/child creating the condition we now call ADHD. And maybe the gremlin has cultivated this form of attack because it works; it gets the gremlin what it is after, negative emotional energy. This is what works with this particular person whereas with someone else it may be depression, GAD or self harming etc.

Each gremlin is different and manifests differently depending on the person that it is manipulating. It then becomes obvious that to alleviate the condition you need to concentrate on releasing the inner gremlin. Eject the irritating inner demons that are the source of the problem. Get rid of the gremlin and in many instances you would get rid of ADHD.

# Chapter 14

## Eating Disorders

Developing an eating disorder is another way your inner gremlin can encourage you to slide into a dysfunctional behaviour pattern designed to trigger your emotions to suit its needs. Anorexia Nervosa, Bulimia and Binge eating are the most common forms and all will have the desired effect of flooding you with negative emotions.

It's the guilt, self hate, anger, frustration, depression and disappointment etc that the gremlin craves. And when you feel these energies surging through your mind and body you are giving the gremlin what it is after. And it is so easy in this day and age with take away food and processed food available everywhere to make the wrong choices. The temptation has never been greater to abuse yourself with food and fall prey to the insatiable parasite within.

The inner demons have never had it so easy to use food to get what they want from you.

If you do experience any form of eating disorder then this is just the way your gremlin has found works with you, it is pushing you in this direction because

**141**

this gets the negative emotions flowing and that is what it needs.

Your gremlin will always search for ways to exploit you and whatever works it will keep repeating over and over. It's up to you to break the cycle and cut off the supply of negativity. It's up to you to truly realise what is happening and to try and turn things around and eject or release the demon within.

Non reaction is the key to not generating the negative emotions and this will weaken the gremlins grip over you. A sensible diet plan will do wonders to thwart the gremlins attempts to get you to abuse yourself in some way with food. Discipline is key to you having a healthy diet to combat the urges from within which are focused on derailing your good intentions.

If you can remain steadfast on your diet for around six weeks this should be long enough to establish new eating habits and reprogram your subconscious mind.

This will break the hold your gremlin may have had over you and help you back up the vibrations to a life without this particular mental health issue causing you problems.

Work on releasing and getting rid of the gremlin and this will lessen the inner desire to slip down the pathway of an eating disorder. Your willpower will

**142**

increase with every step you take in wrestling back control of your mind from the gremlin.

So every time you manage not to react to your thoughts and whatever life throws up at you, you will be releasing a tiny portion of the vibrational essence of your inner gremlin and by the same amount rising in vibration.

# Chapter 15

## Drugs and Alcohol

Growing up is fraught with challenges and it's no surprise that when young adolescents are faced with their first real taste of the stresses of life, that they are drawn to the lure of drugs and alcohol as a way of finding some relief.

They may see it as a way of coping with the emotional upheavals or possibly a cool thing to do because everyone else is doing it.

Whatever the motivation probably most will try it at some point in their teenage years and the majority will only dabble and be able to take it or leave it but for some it will be a different story.

They are the unfortunate one's that seem to be addictive and get hooked and the habit encroaches upon their life in a powerful and destructive way.

So why is it that some can dabble at it maybe for recreational use only and others become addicted and it eats away at them, often tearing their life apart in the process?

I expect if you look closely at the majority of the unfortunate ones that slip in too far,

**144**

you may find most of them have something in common.

And that is an exceptionally powerful inner gremlin.

They will have this more than likely because of a difficult childhood (generally a lack of love in some form) or maybe because of some other trauma they have experienced and this is what makes them different. They have a strong urge for self destruction coming from within and this is what can push them deeply into drugs and alcohol.

These are the young people in danger of addiction and all the terrible consequences that often go hand in hand with that. And it is fuelled by an inner gremlin with a big appetite for negativity.

Another way of describing this bubbling inner anxiety would be, they lack self-love or self-esteem. In other words they are held down in vibration because of the slow vibrating energy of their gremlin. This is why they are prone to feeling not so good about themselves due to the excessive negativity that exists down there.

They are existing in a place where more negativity is present so this will be evident in their life in every respect.

Remember the more powerful the gremlin the more influence it has over you and the more negative energy it needs, so the more damage it will do to your life in the process of getting that energy as it feeds off your emotions.

It will be more active in encouraging you into highly charged emotional states such as angry outbursts, fits of depression even violence and you will feel its inner presence as a simmering ball of anxiety, pulsing its negative energy outwards infecting your thoughts, feelings and emotions.

You could describe it as a feeling of perpetual unhappiness.

This phenomenon is behind many of the mental health problems and sadly in some cases suicides that we see happening in the younger generation today.

Work on releasing the gremlin, making it smaller and in a lot of cases you will have gone a long way towards conquering any addictive tendencies involving drugs and alcohol.

And you will ease the severity of any mental health issues that may be plaguing you and you will lessen the chances of many other mental health problems developing.

**146**

# Chapter 16

## Symptoms

If you suffer from depression, GAD (general anxiety disorder), self harming, ADHD, eating disorders, anger issues, drug or alcohol abuse etc, and it is severe enough to disrupt your life, then you are probably regarded as having a mental illness.

However in the majority of cases these problems are just symptoms of having an overactive powerful inner gremlin.

So it's your gremlin or inner demons that are the real problem.

So when you have therapy or take medication for the symptoms, it's no surprise if it doesn't work too well, when the real answer is sort out the problem. Work on releasing the gremlin is the key and then the symptoms will automatically clear up.

The best way forward is to adopt a mentality of non- reaction. And gain control over your emotions so you stop feeding your gremlin. This self training of your mind will work wonders and the gremlin will weaken as you follow the practice, in turn easing any symptoms you may have.

*'A new simple solution'*

I had quite a lot of inner anger which I managed to cure virtually instantly following this practice.

When I felt the anger stirring within me, my approach focused on deep breathing and repeating the words in my mind 'stay calm' rather than simply allowing the anger to take me over.

Then one day when the anger was stirring and about to surge through me, I managed to hold my focus on my breathing and the powerful energy of anger rushed through my body and whooshed out of the top of my head without taking me over, without engaging me on the way.

That was 15 years ago and I have never felt angry since.

The anger energy left me via the crown chakra and because this energy formed part of my inner gremlin this weakened the gremlin in the process.

This is how you cure the majority of mental health issues by working on releasing the trapped energy that is causing the problem.

# Chapter 17

## Final thoughts

*'A new type of thinking is essential if mankind is to survive and move towards higher levels'*

### -Albert Einstein

This is an interesting choice of words by Professor Einstein, *'move towards higher levels'*, is he talking about energy levels?

What we know for sure is he often talked about the world being energy; this was an important part of his work and formed the basis of much of his thinking.

Why else would anyone say 'levels'?

And *'if mankind is to survive'* must mean he saw something in the future seriously threatening our very existence, could this be referring to the mental health crisis we are currently experiencing?

Bearing in mind that every hurdle and injustice we as humans have to face in our lives is created by ourselves, whilst under the negative influence of our inner gremlin. So essentially we are through whatever mental health state we are in, contributing to the mess the world is in right now.

**149**

It's a reflection of our collective mental health state, and we are without doubt, currently existing in a lower level version of the world.

And finally his reference to *'a new type of thinking'* could certainly be talking about high vibrational thinking, as this is thinking from the awareness of everything being energy and this automatically encourages thinking more positively.

It is also a new refreshing way to look at the world and can be very revealing and empowering in many ways.

It certainly seems to fit with what Einstein was saying and if the world did adopt this way of thinking and actually encouraged people to work together to release their inner gremlins then, it would move mankind up to a new level.

And this would be a higher vibrational level, where negative energy would not be able to influence and damage us so easily, therefore immediately changing the world for the better.

This would make it a more positively orientated existence, abundant with more high vibrational energies such as love, joy, peace, kindness, sincerity, and happiness etc. This would then become our new default setting, our new natural state of being.

Lots of the more negative stuff such as anger, hate, envy, greed, jealousy, selfishness and fear etc, would fall away because these energies would be too slow vibrating to survive in such a high vibrational world.

And it would be a place where the mental health crisis could not exist in the way it is today because it is a manifestation only possible in a lower vibrational world.

Food for thought.

## Other recommended books and videos:

**High Vibrational Thinking**, the power to change your life, Author Steve Wharton, Amazon Kindle

**Feeding your demons**, Author Tsultrim Allione, Hay House Publishing

**The Power of Now**, Author Eckhart Tolle, Namaste Publishing

**The Emotion Code**, Author Bradley Nelson, Penguin Publishing

**The Secret**, Author Rhonda Byrne, Thorsons/Simon & Schuster UK

**The most important years of a child's life**, Author Steve Wharton, Amazon Kindle

**Bullying Stops Here**, Author Steve Wharton, Amazon Kindle

**The Power of Non-resistance**, Author Steve Wharton, Amazon Kindle

Videos:
**E-motion the movie**
**www.e-motionthemovie.com**

*'A new simple solution'*

## Useful Resources UK

**Samaritans**. To talk about anything that is upsetting you, you can contact Samaritans 24 hours a day, 365 days a year. You can call 116 123 (free from any phone), email jo@samaritans.org or visit some branches in person. You can also call the Samaritans Welsh Language Line on 0808 164 0123 (7pm–11pm every day).

**SANEline**. If you're experiencing a mental health problem or supporting someone else, you can call SANEline on 0300 304 7000 (4.30pm–10.30pm every day).

**National Suicide Prevention Helpline** UK. Offers a supportive listening service to anyone with thoughts of suicide. You can call the National Suicide Prevention Helpline UK on 0800 689 5652 (6pm to midnight every day).

**Campaign Against Living Miserably** (CALM). You can call the CALM on 0800 58 58 58 (5pm–midnight every day) if you are struggling and need to talk. Or if you prefer not to speak on the phone, you could try the CALM webchat service.

**Shout**. If you would prefer not to talk but want some mental health support, you could text SHOUT to 85258. Shout offers a confidential 24/7 text service providing support if you are in crisis and need immediate help.

**The Mix**. If you're under 25, you can call The Mix on <u>0808 808 4994</u> (3pm–midnight every day), request support by email <u>using this form on The Mix website</u> or <u>use their crisis text messenger service</u>.

**Papyrus HOPELINEUK**. If you're under 35 and struggling with suicidal feelings, or concerned about a young person who might be struggling, you can call <u>Papyrus HOPELINEUK</u> on <u>0800 068 4141</u> (weekdays 10am-10pm, weekends 2pm-10pm and bank holidays 2pm–10pm), email <u>pat@papyrus-uk.org</u> or text <u>07786 209 697</u>.

**Nightline.** If you're a student, you can look on the <u>Nightline website</u> to see if your university or college offers a night-time listening service. Nightline phone operators are all students too.

**Switchboard.** If you identify as gay, lesbian, bisexual or transgender, you can call <u>Switchboard</u> on <u>0300 330 0630</u> (10am–10pm every day), email <u>chris@switchboard.lgbt</u> or use their webchat service. Phone operators all identify as LGBT+.

**C.A.L.L.** If you live in Wales, you can call <u>the Community Advice and Listening Line (C.A.L.L.)</u> on <u>0800 132 737</u> (open 24/7) or you can text 'help' followed by a question to 81066.

**Helplines Partnership**. For more options, visit <u>the Helplines Partnership</u> website for a directory of UK helplines. <u>Mind's Infoline</u> can also help you find services that can support you. If you're outside the UK, the <u>Befrienders Worldwide</u> website has a tool to search by country for emotional support helplines around the world.

**Urgent mental health helplines (England only)**
If you live in England, you can call a local NHS urgent mental health helpline for support during a mental health crisis. Anyone can call these helplines, at any time.

*'A new simple solution'*

Printed by Amazon Italia Logistica S.r.l.
Torrazza Piemonte (TO), Italy

53866360R00090